I Call You Friends

I Call You Friends

John Cavadini and the Vision of Catholic Leadership
for Higher Education

Edited by
LEONARD J. DeLORENZO
and TIMOTHY P. O'MALLEY

PICKWICK *Publications* · Eugene, Oregon

I CALL YOU FRIENDS
John Cavadini and the Vision of Catholic Leadership for Higher Education

Pickwick Publications
An Imprint of Wipf and Stock Publishers
199 W. 8th Ave., Suite 3
Eugene, OR 97401

www.wipfandstock.com

PAPERBACK ISBN: 978-1-5326-5459-6
HARDCOVER ISBN: 978-1-5326-5460-2
EBOOK ISBN: 978-1-5326-5461-9

Cataloguing-in-Publication data:

Names: DeLorenzo, Leonard J., editor. | O'Malley, Timothy P., editor

Title: I call you friends : John Cavadini and the vision of Catholic leadership for higher education / edited by Leonard J. DeLorenzo and Timothy P. O'Malley.

Description: Eugene, OR : Pickwick Publications, 2019 | Includes bibliographical references.

Identifiers: ISBN 978-1-5326-5459-6 (paperback) | ISBN 978-1-5326-5460-2 (hardcover) | ISBN 978-1-5326-5461-9 (ebook)

Subjects: LCSH: Cavadini, John C. | Catholic universities and colleges—United States. | Catholic Church—Education (Higher)—United States. | Catholic universities and colleges—United States—Administration.

Classification: LC501 .I17 2019 (paperback) | LC501 .I17 (ebook)

Manufactured in the U.S.A.   05/22/19

Contents

List of Contributors

Ann W. Astell, PhD, is Professor of Theology and Director of Undergraduate Studies at the University of Notre Dame. Her publications include *Eating Beauty: The Eucharist and the Spiritual Arts of the Middle Ages, Joan of Arc and Sacrificial Authorship*, and *The Song of Songs in the Middle Ages.*

Stephen M. Barr, PhD, is Professor of Physics and Astronomy at the University of Delaware, as well as President of the Society of Catholic Scientists. In addition to numerous scholarly articles in his field, his publications include *Modern Science and Ancient Faith, Science and Religion: The Myth of Conflict*, and *The Believing Scientist.*

Leonard J. DeLorenzo, PhD, is Director of Undergraduate Studies and Academic Director of Notre Dame Vision in the McGrath Institute for Church Life with a concurrent appointment in the department of theology at the University of Notre Dame. His publications include *Witness: Learning to Tell the Stories of Grace that Illumine Our Lives, Work of Love: A Theological Reconstruction of the Communion of Saints*, and *What Matters Most.*

John Garvey, JD, is President of the Catholic University of America. His publications include *Religion and the Constitution, Sexuality and the U.S. Catholic Church*, and *The First Amendment.*

Michael Heintz, PhD, is a priest of the Diocese of Fort Wayne–South Bend and Associate Professor of Historical and Systematic Theology at Mount St. Mary's University. He is the author of many scholarly articles.

Peter Kilpatrick, PhD, is Provost of the Illinois Institute of Technology and former Dean of the College of Engineering at the University of Notre Dame. He is the author of more than 100 refereed journal articles.

Melanie M. Morey, EdD, recently retired as director of the Office of Catholic Identity Assessment and Formation and associate superintendent of the Archdiocese of San Francisco. Her publications include *Higher Education: A Culture in Crisis* and *Renewing Parish Culture: Building for a Catholic Future.*

Francesca Aran Murphy, PhD, is Professor of Theology at the University of Notre Dame. She is the author of *Art and Intellect in the Philosophy of Étienne Gilson, The Comedy of Revelation,* and *Christ the Form of Beauty,* among other publications.

Timothy P. O'Malley, PhD, is Director of Education and Academic Director of the Center for Liturgy in the McGrath Institute for Church Life with a concurrent appointment in the department of theology at the University of Notre Dame. He is the author of *Liturgy and the New Evangelization, Bored Again Catholic,* and *Off the Hook: God, Love, Dating, and Marriage in a Hookup World*

Cyril O'Regan, PhD, is the Catherine Huisking Professor of Theology at the University of Notre Dame. His publications include *Anatomy of Misremembering, Theology and the Spaces of the Apocalyptic, Gnostic Apocalypse,* and *The Heterodox Hegel.*

Rasoul Rasoulipour, PhD, is Associate Professor of Philosophy of Religion and Dean of Faculty in the School of Letters and Humanities at the University of Kharazmi. His publications include *Science and Religion in Quest of Truth, Hume's Natural Religion: Rereading Hume's 'Dialogues concerning Natural Religion,'* and *Sacredness of the Other, Love and Healing.*

Gabriel Said Reynolds, PhD, is Professor of Islamic Studies and Theology at the University of Notre Dame. His publications include *The Qur'an and the Bible, The Emergence of Islam,* and *The Qur'an and its Biblical Subtext.*

Most Rev. Kevin C. Rhoades is the Bishop of the Diocese of Fort Wayne-South Bend and chairman of the USCCB committee on doctrine.

Carolyn Y. Woo, PhD is the Distinguished President's Fellow for Global Development at Purdue University, as well as the former CEO of Catholic Relief Services (2012–2016) and Dean of the Mendoza College of Business at the University of Notre Dame (1997–2011).

Most Rev. Allen Vigneron is the Archbishop of Detroit, secretary of the United States Conference of Catholic Bishops, and former chairman of USCCB committee on doctrine.

Introduction

THIS VOLUME IS DEDICATED to John Cavadini with a title taken from the words Jesus speaks to his disciples. It is audacious to apply such a title, but none other seems so appropriate. It is appropriate precisely because of what Jesus means when he says these words during his long farewell discourse, and we shall say more about this momentarily. But it is also appropriate because anyone—we mean *anyone*—who has ever sat in a class John Cavadini has taught, attended lectures he has given or hosted, or been part of a meeting over which he has presided knows that he always begins in the same way: he calls us "friends."

Jesus calls his disciples "friends" because they are being called to rely on him—on his word—and to make a pledge of themselves to what cannot be seen or proven, but must be trusted. John Cavadini asks for the same trust not in *himself* or in *his* word, but rather in the testimony of Christ, who continues to ask us to make a gift of ourselves and lean not on our own understanding (see Prov 3:5–6; John 20:29; 1 Pet 1:8).

That this greeting has become habitual for Cavadini and familiar to his students and colleagues increases rather than diminishes its significance: what he invites others into is always—*always*—a space of friendship. It is a space of suspending disbelief and striving together to reach for communion especially amid those things that seem bound to separate. That this is his common greeting in a university environment is more significant still, for here the powers of hidden agendas and splintering paradigms hide under the cover of supposed sophistication to strain the fundamental act of trust that is necessary for pursuing truth as a communal endeavor. This is where he calls us "friends."

The Catholic university, first of all, is charged with the mission of seeking truth for its own sake, with a bedrock conviction about who holds all things together as one. The Catholic university seeks peace, not as the world promises peace, but as the lasting gift of a sacrifice made for others. The Catholic university is thus a school of charity, where scholarship and teaching are at once forms of healing, discovery, and service, ordered to the one who is the "power and wisdom of God" (1 Cor 1:24).

When John Cavadini calls us "friends," he beckons us to join him in a space of bringing together those very things that seem to be irremediably separate. As we will read in this volume, this includes the healing and re-union of such fractures as those between science and religion, theology and business, Eucharistic worship and social justice, stewardship and Catholic mission, the Church and Islam, holiness and scholarship. What Cavadini lends to these divisions and perceived rivalries is nothing short of a holistic Catholic vision: a vision of the whole, a vision of beauty, a vision hope, a vision of communion, a vision of mission founded in and ordered to Christ.

The Catholic vision is neither a vision of compromise nor of intransigence; it is a vision of charity. Compromise might require you to become less yourself to meet someone else who is also becoming less themselves. Intransigence is born of hubris and self-focus. Charity lets the other be other, while seeking a bond through actions of bearing witness, listening deeply, dialoguing, studying, and praying. Charity is an act of trust, most of all to the one who gives his own Spirit as the guarantee of charity's validity.

This Catholic vision as charity is not something, therefore, that Cavadini simply purveys or heralds; rather, it is something to which he gives personal testimony as administrator, teacher, mentor, and public intellectual. He is, himself, in his person, a healer. Because of the power of his Catholic vision, he can and does disagree with people, sometimes strongly. But he never fails in charity. Among everyone, he is kindest to those who might otherwise seem on some occasion or another to be his adversaries. He shows what it actually means to love those with whom you are at odds, seeking their good and conferring honor on them. He calls them "friends," too.

We endeavored to bring this volume together because, quite frankly, Cavadini's vision of leadership in Catholic higher education is too bright and too necessary to be overlooked, but at the same time it is often difficult to see as a whole. It is difficult to see precisely because of its range and comprehensiveness. After spending more than a decade within the McGrath Institute for Church Life under his leadership, we have witnessed the splendor of this vision firsthand. Even still, we are not alone in feeling like we are always trying to catch up with the vision, seeing with him to its furthest horizons, and continually rediscovering the Gospel with wonder and gratitude in the modes of scholarship and service.

The contributors to this volume have provided perspectives unto the breadth and depth of this vision of Catholic leadership for higher education, with the hope that, together in the spirit of friendship, we can offer a true but non-exhaustive witness to this distinctive form of leadership that Cavadini embodies. Some of the essays that follow are explicitly about Cavadini's vision and achievements to date, while others are offered in dedication to him on topics for which he himself continues to provide leadership. This leadership has never been more necessary for the life of the Catholic university and its service to the Church.

As editors of this volume, we have been privileged in receiving the riches of this education into leadership over the years from our teacher, mentor, and now boss. We have seen him give learned papers that challenge prevailing scholarly narratives, unmasking discourses of power through a gentleness that few scholars possess. We have seen him give advice during office hours to undergraduates on discerning their vocation in the same afternoon that he has counseled bishops on complicated pastoral matters. We have seen him educate not only in the august halls of the university but also in his living room where he has invited students and visitors to learn the nature of Christian charity as it is performed in the home.

John Cavadini fulfills the ideal of the theologian that Pope Francis describes in his *Evangelii Gaudium*. Cavadini is most assuredly *not* a desk-bound theologian–he is at once scholar and evangelizer, servant and leader, disciple and mentor, teacher and witness.[1] Despite an active teaching and research load, he is ever-ready to heed the needs of the Church and to assist the university in its mission to serve the Church. This has led him to orchestrate pastoral initiatives with the African bishops' conference, to provide theological education in China, and to collaborate for the sake of promoting vocations among African American Catholics. He has organized and sponsored conferences on timely and insightful topics like the charism of priestly celibacy, interreligious dialogue through the witness of holy persons from various traditions, new pedagogies for teaching science and religion in Catholic secondary schools, Marian theology and devotion on the eve of the Second Vatican Council, and the evangelization of young people today, to name a few. When he is not leading an initiative himself, he is just as likely to address the USCCB on priorities for the New

1. See Francis, *Evangelii Gaudium*, 133–34.

Evangelization as he is to spend a weekend delivering a retreat on conse-crated life to cloistered nuns.

For his tireless labors to date, the Church and the academy have already bestowed auspicious honors on him. To name but a few of these honors: Pope Benedict XVI recognized Cavadini's outstanding service to the Church in general and the Holy See in particular by naming him to the Equestrian Order of St. Gregory the Great, *classis civilis*. Pope Benedict XVI also appointed Cavadini to the International Theological Commission, on which he served from 2009–2013, while he currently serves as an advi-sor to the doctrine committee of the USCCB. Furthermore, in addition to numerous teaching awards at Notre Dame and elsewhere, in February 2018 he received the Monica K. Helwig Award for Outstanding Contributions to Catholic Intellectual Life. What is recognized from the confines of his own classrooms to the halls of the Holy See is that Cavadini's service to the academy and the Church is unfailingly given with a full heart, with the utmost care and wisdom, and for the greater glory of God.

Readers of Augustine will understand where Cavadini learned the gift of educating each and every person from the heart of the Church. Writing to the deacon Deogratis, who finds himself bored addressing those new to Christian life, Augustine reminds:

> If our understanding finds its delight within, in the brightest of secret places, let it also delight in the following insight into the ways of love: the more love goes down in a spirit of service into the ranks of the lowliest people, the more surely it rediscovers the quiet that is within when its good conscience testifies that it seeks nothing of those to whom it goes down but their eternal salvation.[2]

Cavadini improves a bit on St. Augustine's claim. For Cavadini, spend-ing an afternoon with seventh graders in confirmation or teaching 250 stu-dents in a course on the Catholic faith is not a matter of encountering the "lowliest people." For him, each and every person matters in the act of edu-cation. Each and every person can ascend to the heights of contemplation through an encounter with an educator who cares. And as one sees in Ca-vadini's own teaching, as he explains something he has nonetheless taught a thousand times, he seems as delighted with the insight into divine love as if he himself were learning it for the first time. His style of teaching is noth-ing less than a pedagogy of encounter where students come to see how the great doctrines of Christianity are not reducible to abstract formulations

2. Augustine, *Instructing Beginners in Faith*, I.10.15.

Introduction

about the triunity of God but are instead answers to the great questions of life: What is love? What is happiness? How can I learn gratitude?

In his preaching at the University of Notre Dame, the late Bishop John Michael D'Arcy would inevitably mention the name of John Cavadini in his litany of Notre Dame legends: Blessed Basil Moreau, Fr. Edward Sorin, Fr. Ted Hesburgh, and John Cavadini. Although John would never be comfortable with us saying it, when the history of Notre Dame in the late twentieth and early twentieth-first century is written, he will have more than a chapter in it. As Fr. Hesburgh himself communicated before his death in 2015, John's appointment as head of the McGrath Institute for Church Life was one of the most important things that has happened at Notre Dame in its modern history.

It continues to be our great privilege to receive mentorship from this theologian, this leader in Catholic education, this friend. And the hope is that this volume will facilitate an encounter with Cavadini's leadership for the benefit of all in higher education.

Leonard J. DeLorenzo
Timothy P. O'Malley

March 19, 2019
Solemnity of Saint Joseph

PART 1

Leadership in Charity:
Born from the Heart

1

John Cavadini
and the Catholic University

Cyril O'Regan

IN NORTH AMERICA OVER the last three decades no one has thought as long and hard about the nature of the Catholic university, has been so passionate in its avowal, so visionary in its conception, and so persistent in reminding all that would listen that the university is a specifically Catholic achievement and the *Catholic* university an enduring legacy as John Cavadini. It is also true to say that that no Catholic voice has been quite so multidimensional and ramified in articulating the Catholic university's various requirements at the level of administration, faculty, students, as well as its various structures in terms of the role and function of the Department of Theology or Religious Studies department, the curriculum, and the internal and external programming that is both the Catholic university's expression and life-blood. Over the years this great Augustine scholar and teacher has demonstrated the singular ability to present the Catholic tradition with freshness and currency, while convincingly elucidating the compatibility of reason in its deepest and broadest expanse to a faith considered not as a burden, but as a gift that is truly a light that directs, sustains, and fructifies. If there has been some frustration, there has been more success; if there have been setbacks, none has essentially detracted from the persuasiveness of the claim made or dulled the eloquence of its expression in talks, in articles, in conferences with leaders, college presidents, and bishops all of whom it appears need to be convinced at some point or another, or for one reason or another, that a Catholic university is not an oxymoron, that faith is truly compatible with reason, and that, indeed, in line with the visionary first part of *Ex corde* that the Catholic university is the privileged site of communion where intellect probes deeply and expansively, and where faith actively seeks the understanding that is its aim and responsibility.

Even those who have not been entirely persuaded by John Cavadini's vision would admit that it is inspirational. This pays homage to the surprising eloquence of a palpably reticent individual who over his career as a theologian has proven himself to be a consummate listener, and whose facility for both admiring and praising others knows no bounds. Very few academics have learned the lesson that he believes his beloved Augustine has taught all of us, that is, to say "thank you" to each other and, of course, God. Like Henri de Lubac and Benedict XVI before him, Cavadini also reminds us to say "thank you" to the tradition or *traditio* of the Church in all its intellectual, affective, liturgical, and practical forms. This gratitude is at once rare and profoundly appropriate since tradition is the 'handing over' and 'handing on' that is itself a protracted 'thank you' to the triune God for the gift of salvation and for the gift of showing us the way in and through Christ how we might let ourselves be formed by and conformed to love that is spelled out over the course of our lives.

In this reflection I would like to bring out not so much John Cavadini's eloquence as the integral nature of his vision that in its general form rises high above what passes for understanding the Catholic university and in its fully articulated form demonstrates a fundamental coherence that is unrivalled in our time. Ours is indeed a time that is marked equally by intemperance and lack of conviction, and tempted, on the one hand, to disengage from the broader culture and become sectarian and, on the other, to capitulate entirely to the secular culture's understanding of reason and its ambition to attenuate and sanitize faith. Cavadini's is truly the third way of confident Catholic presentation and self-presentation and real and vulnerable engagement with all that is true, good and beautiful in the world, in knowing, practice and form of life, although he would be the very first to admit that the third way is already outlined in the two documents on the Church at Vatican II, *Lumen Gentium* and *Gaudium et Spes*, or more precisely the relationship between them. I will not attempt to demonstrate this coherence in all of its aspects and complications. I will limit myself simply to bringing out some of its more salient elements. In addition, rather than produce the book of evidence, to cite the when and where of a particular aspect of Cavadini's thought, or focus on a particular nuance, I will confine myself to presenting the essential properties of those features of John Cavadini's thinking that are under discussion and to tease out their relations. I have in mind among other things John Cavadini's reflections on the Catholic mission of the university, the proprietors of the mission, the role of a theology department in the university with its manifest obligations as well as rights, and whether and how the Catholic university can help the Church.

DOUBLE INTERVENTION

But before I do any of this, I think it incumbent on me to situate John Cavadini's vision as a double intervention. First, and most broadly, his vision is an intervention into the secular academic landscape of North America in which faith is regarded as prime species of obscurantism and overzealousness with an inbuilt tilt towards fanaticism. Second, it is an intervention into the ongoing discussion in Catholic institutions of higher learning in which all too often the basic operative premise is that with all the good will in the world, prestige and faith commitment in the end have to be conceived as a zero-sum game. Since prestige is the more patent of the two goods, and specifically the one more comprehensible to a Board of Trustees, it is no surprise that routinely the institutional witness to Catholic faith gets short shrift.

I will return shortly to the point of the downplaying of Catholic faith and speak to the ways in which Catholic colleges and universities often tend to compensate for this fact and thereby disguise it. But first, under pain of blurring the distinction between John Cavadini and Alasdair MacIntyre, it should be said that in the case of John Cavadini the second intervention is focal and explicit, whereas the diagnostics concerning the effect of secular rationality on the self-understanding of the university in general and the Catholic university in particular is more nearly implied. Still, there is much in the articles and talks that John Cavadini has given on the Catholic university that supposes MacIntyre's analysis of the distorting effect on the self-understanding of the university exercised by the authority of secular rationality, whereby the university comes to think of itself as exclusively promoting demonstrable professional expertise useful to the broader society from which it has taken a long and perhaps questionable holiday. This too should not surprise. Both MacIntyre and Cavadini are students of John Henry Newman, and Newman's singular genius was that at one and the same time he uncovered the biases of secular reason as it arrogated to itself absolute authority in uncovering biases and prejudices in religion while ignoring its own, and argued not only that a Catholic university is not a contradiction in terms, but is in fact the site in which reason properly understood could flourish and faith engage in the kind of self-examination that is proper to it, indeed, nothing short of an obligation.

MacIntyre's energies are more focused on resisting the authority of the operative model of secular reason and questioning its scope. Consequently, he limits himself to producing a mere sketch of the institutional and curricular implications regarding our understanding of the university, although he has suggested enough that would question thinking of undergraduate education after the model of graduate education which can rightly be regarded as the acquisition of expertise in a particular discipline. For example, the very notion of undergraduate research would seem questionable to him and supplant the primary good of learning how to ask the right kind of question, which in MacIntyre's view is the indelible sign of intellectual excellence. In contrast, Cavadini's immediate focus is on the incoherence so obviously manifest in Catholic universities regarding mission, organization, and curriculum and only indirectly on the operation of secular reason, which with MacIntyre he recognizes is by no means as neutral regarding faith as it claims to be, basically constructing faith as interfering with free inquiry and prescribing something like a *noli me tangere* when it comes to reason's relation to faith.

This is to say that MacIntyre and Cavadini are focused on different sides of the complex problem of secular modernity unveiled by Newman in the nineteenth century. As a traditional thinker and not simply a thinker of tradition, John Cavadini has ever before him such works as the encyclical *Fides et Ratio* (1998) and the apostolic constitution *Ex corde ecclesia* (2002), which in a sense unite together the two dimensions of the complex problem diagnosed by, but also dealt with by, Newman in his classic *The Idea of the University* (1865) and *An Essay in Aid of a Grammar of Assent* (1870). Remarkably, in the case of both texts Newman not only provides diagnoses of where things have gone wrong, but offers genuine hope that reason can be rehabilitated, and more specifically that the counterfeit of reason that has ditched presuppositions, precisely those that will guide it regarding its search for truth, can give way to a form of reason that is accepting of presupposition and ample and flexible in its mode of reasoning such that it does not block its natural inclination to appreciate transcendent truths that cannot be demonstrated. The repatriation of this form of reason can help guide the Church in the ongoing task of being true to itself in a changing world as well as in its dialogue with the world. But in a particular way repatriation finds its locus in the university and especially in the Catholic university. While understanding the magnitude of the challenges that face the Church and the Catholic university, much like Benedict XVI, who has after Newman heroically argued for a ampler notion of reason and for that possibility because of the actuality of the communion between faith and reason, John Cavadini's vision is a vision of hope.

If the language of John Cavadini occasionally strikes one as prophetic, there is nothing Cassandra-like about its tone not to mention its substance. If there is an imperative and thus a "must," the accent falls on "can." For John Cavadini, while the scene of Catholic universities and colleges might at first blush be characterized by confusion and lack of will, on further inspection there is much that promises a less confused and more determinately Catholic future. A crisis—and we may be experiencing a crisis—is not the same thing as a calamitous failure. There are a number of inspiring college presidents and higher administrators, many examples of well-meaning bishops who understand the complexities of a Catholic university that has responsibilities both to the Catholic tradition and free inquiry and compelled to negotiate the tension between them, any number of heroic faculty who put personal ambition aside for the common good of the Catholic university, and significant evidence of substantial buy-in by students to the mission and goals of a Catholic university. Cavadini is liberal in his praise of small liberal arts Catholic colleges that not only provide a strong 'Catholic' education, but a rich 'catholic' education. Nor does he lack sympathy for Catholic institutions that due to market forces feel compelled to downplay the integral disciplines of theology and philosophy and constitute themselves as niche institutions that survive by specializing in nursing, business, or continuing education. The relevant Catholic actors are for him Catholic institutions that are relatively solvent either because of endowment, enrollment, or both. Such institutions, he believes, bear the responsibility of constructing a Catholic university where the adjective truly qualifies the noun. As already hinted, his discourse regarding the Catholic university is not prescriptive in the strict sense in that he avoids couching the issue of a Catholic university in the language of "ought" that is almost always desperate. The register of Cavadini is more nearly descriptive. Given the venerable tradition of the Catholic university and all the positive signs noted above, there is no reason not to expect progress—albeit fragile progress—in the making and remaking of the Catholic university that not only tolerates but encourages the elevation of both faith and reason.

MISSION: INSPIRATION AND IMAGINATION

No one recognizes as well as John Cavadini that the mission of the Catholic university or college is not always captured in a mission statement. Mission statements tend to be formulaic and are routinely worded in a manner that takes precautions against any suggestion of sectarian exclusion. A particular university or college can be much more deeply Catholic in its institutional arrangements, its curriculum and programming, its Campus Ministry, and in its outreach than its mission statement might suggest. Of course, it can also fall below, sometimes significantly below the sentiments expressed in its mission statement.

Granting all of this, John Cavadini does think that mission statements matter. Allowing for the constraints on mission statements stated above, they can be vacuous or determinate; they can deaden or inspire. It is not sufficient then, for example, to say that the Catholic university has as its mission peace or justice. These commendable goals are also the goals of secular universities and colleges as well as often being the stated goals of contestants in beauty pageants. Without some more determinate reference to Catholicism, they function vacuously. And it is John Cavadini's basic intuition that when the goals are indeterminate, they fail to inspire and excite the imagination. Thirty-five years in higher education have convinced him that what is needed above all in Catholic universities and colleges is inspiration. In the case above, the goals of peace and justice are truly Catholic goals only if, on the one hand, they are the fruit of the ongoing reflection of the Church on the world that it is embedded in and with which it relates in conversation and responsible argument and, on the other, that the goals of peace and justice are connected in the figure of Christ who is witnessed to in the New Testament and anticipated in the Hebrew scriptures, and has a fundamental place in liturgy. For him Catholic Social Teaching is itself the fruit of the Church's reflection on the mystery of salvation in Christ and on the Christian life in which social action is the correlative of worship and prayer and vice versa.

Ideally, mission statements of Catholic universities and colleges should reflect this holistic view that Cavadini has found to be so inspiring both in classrooms at Notre Dame and the creative programs of outreach that contribute to the new evangelization that he and his incredibly talented collaborators at the McGrath Institute for Church Life have constructed and developed over the years. These years have brought with it the wisdom that the least common denominator does not give life, elevate, engender and sustain purpose. What succeeds in doing all of this, what makes a Catholic university a place of inspiration is to aim higher, to take on the challenge of being different as well as open, and in particular to offer to the world of universities a very particular light that it does not have.

If it seems that Cavadini has had this holistic conception of the Catholic university from the beginning of his career, and thus this view has been his as a matter of Catholic instinct, this does not mean that he has not found support, direction, and inspiration in the broad Catholic tradition. Of course, one has to mention Augustine and not only for the reason that *de doctrina Christiana* is one of the great texts focused on the relation of Catholicism to secular knowledge and culture. One of Notre Dame's worst kept secrets is that John Cavadini is not only a great teacher of Augustine, but a veritable phenomenon when it comes to speaking of the great theologian who was preeminently teacher, priest, bishop, and saint. In the classroom and in his articles Cavadini has displayed the uncanny ability to channel Augustine, and make him speak—sometimes apparently directly—to our current condition, to the crisis in Catholic education as well as the crises in our understanding of sex and marriage, to the vexing questions of how to define church as irreducible to mere organization while holding it accountable, and to how the church enters passionately into the world with all its sufferings and searching as well as complexities and confusion while having a more comprehensive mission. Perhaps closer to home, however, support has been provided by the abundant and nourishing thought of Benedict XVI, whose work was the subject of a conference put on by John Cavadini a number of years ago at Notre Dame and which led to a distinguished volume that he edited and eventually had the opportunity to present to the Pope in person for the celebration of his 85th birthday.

What Benedict XVI has written over the years both as Pope and in the years preceding his Pontificate as Joseph Ratzinger has proved tonic whether regarding the essential unity of faith and reason; the Augustinian take on the essential nature of theology being faith seeking understanding; the insistence that Catholic social teaching both begins and ends in Christ insofar as the goal is the kingdom of God; exhortations regarding the continual importance of the saints as icons of the icon of Christ, as teachers of the Catholic faith and abiding models of Christian excellence made possible by grace; and the abiding sense of scripture as being a text like no other, as being nothing less than unfolding the mystery of salvation as a story that includes the readers and in consequence demanding not only all our textual diligence but also all the resources of our creativity and imagination. And one final gift: perhaps more than any other Catholic thinker in the past decades, Benedict XVI has advanced the view of the Catholic university as the place of responsible questioning and listening that upholds the Augustinian distinction between wisdom and knowledge, that encourages investigation of the presuppositions of faith while also demanding that one not leave unexamined secular assumptions about knowledge and the good life that rarely get examined, and in significant respects have become immunized from questioning and criticism.

As noted previously, however, there is not a one-to-one correspondence between the mission statement of a Catholic university or college and its execution of the mission. Just as a determinate and potentially inspiring mission statement may be effectively inoperative because of lack of leadership, dearth of talented and motivated faculty, and inadequacies in curriculum, a less than inspiring mission statement can be compensated for by true leadership, talented faculty, and a curriculum that is realistically but substantively Catholic. Importantly, however, on Cavadini's account all three are indispensable. I will speak to just one here.

Leadership at the level of president, provost, and dean is essential to the well-being of a Catholic university and college. Leaders need to have not only managerial skills and financial competence, they need to have a vision of what gives their institution purpose as well as definition, what kind of faculty they are looking for, what emphases they are going to place on research and teaching, and a sense of coherence in curriculum that convinces in the long term—if not necessarily the short term. Translated into the idiom of Alasdair MacIntyre, John Cavadini thinks that leaders in a Catholic university or college ideally are marked by forms of intellectual and moral excellence that is exhibited in judgment. No more here than elsewhere has John Cavadini mouthed pieties regarding leadership. He has brought presidents and trustees from Catholic universities and colleges together to converse and think with each other regarding the definition of the Catholic university and also on the more practical matters of remaining financially viable as these colleges face the headwinds of an increasingly challenging higher education market, are forced to consider the price to be paid for accepting government monies, feel the need to ask questions about the curriculum without succumbing to the axiom that change is the only permissible outcome because the only permissible good, establish programming that will excite but at the same time enhance the Catholic mission of the university or college, and give due attention to the faith life of the students. And, of course, without the mantle of president, provost, or even dean, John Cavadini too has been a leader, indeed, an extraordinary one. In addition to the power of judgment that can see and cut the Gordian knot of difficulties, leaders in a Catholic university and college require real courage. In this regard, in his capacities as Chair of the Department of Theology at Notre Dame and Director of the McGrath Institute for Church Life, John Cavadini has been as singular in his courage as in his wisdom.

THE DEPARTMENT OF THEOLOGY
AND HOW IT MATTERS

Being Chair of the Department of Theology at Notre Dame did not create the conviction in John Cavadini that it is essential to the enactment of the mission of the Catholic university. Rather it confirmed it. Of course, there are obvious conditions for that to be true. The following in no particular order is a mere distillation of what John Cavadini has said far more eloquently, capaciously, and hauntingly over the years. (1) That the department of Theology should be regarded by the Catholic university as central to its self-understanding and mission and that the department's own self-understanding is that it is an integrative discipline that attends to the unity of knowledge. The latter is the unique aspiration of the Catholic university. This is not to say that the mission of the Catholic university is housed in the Theology department. The mission is shared by the different colleges and departments and to succeed a Catholic university requires that the rights and obligations of the mission are shared by all. At the same time, however, such a responsibility is most intentionally the responsibility of the Department of Theology. (2) The Department of Theology is itself a multi-disciplinary entity in turn open to all institutional forms of learning.

If within itself it serves as the curator of the disciplines of philology, history, ethics, and even to some extent philosophy as these ultimately are brought to bear on the deposit of faith, essentially it values all the disciplines, those of the natural and social sciences as well as the Humanities as contributing to our understanding of human being, the world, and that reality that gives to each its ultimate meaning. (3) The shared understanding of all the members of a Department of Theology is that whatever their particular area of expertise 'faith seeking understanding' provides the overall horizon within which each faculty member engages or enacts the discipline of Theology or one of its many sub-disciplines, even if there are more immediate goals and more proximate horizons of inquiry. (4) While the autonomy of inquiry is to be upheld, nonetheless, there is the expectation that the theological and magisterial traditions will be treated with respect. (5) The Department of Theology should both expect and recognize intellectual excellence in scholarship and theological inquiry, while also recognizing excellence in teaching. Beyond these truisms, it is necessary to have an appreciation for the different excellences such that the department as a whole exceeds the sum of its parts. These may also include programming as well as research and teaching. Although not uniquely located in the Chair of the department, such appreciation and the accompanying judgment as to what combination of excellences and gifts is necessary for the department to flourish and to enable its fulfillment of its particular mission in the university is held in trust by the Chair.

The above barely touches on the wise council provided by John Cavadini regarding the nature and function of the Catholic university, and in fact amounts to far less than the distillation I promised. I do, however, want to say a little more about the necessities of high intellect and quality teaching. Still, before I do so, I should touch on a conundrum. What are the responsibilities of the Theology department when it appears either that administration is confused or careless regarding mission and cavalier regarding the role Theology plays in the curriculum? In the former case, to the extent to which it is functioning properly, the Department of Theology can help to advise, clarify, disambiguate, and fortify the mission of the university; in the latter case the department not only can but has the responsibility to protest despite the prospect of being seen to be shrill and self-interested. A department can and should be criticized for not carrying out its mission. At the same time it ought not to be the object of disdain because it is doing precisely what it is charged with doing, that is, lifting up an immensely rich two thousand year tradition of faith and inquiry, worship and forms of life in the hope that this tradition can contribute to the challenging questions of the day, but also to the perennial questions about meaning and truth, about goodness and beauty that seem the special behest and prerogatives of human beings. To return to the intellectual excellence and excellence in teaching that John Cavadini believes is sponsored by a properly functioning Department of Theology—it is a view shared by the early Church Fathers, Aquinas, Newman, and Benedict XVI that properly functioning intellect—that is, an intellect genuinely oriented towards the truth and not riddled by pride or ambition—is an intrinsic good. It is a good, moreover, that is not inimical to faith, since there is the shared faith in reason as having the capacity to open out onto faith and its reception of Christ, who is the Truth. Thus, John Cavadini's basic conviction is very much in line with what is a Catholic consensus.

For John Cavadini, this is no mere Scholastic deduction. He understands well that the value placed on high intellect serves the reputation of the department both within the university and outside. He worries, however, about confounding high intellect with prestige. While Catholic universities should necessarily avoid parochialism and special pleading on behalf of its faculty, it should also have the confidence in its own abilities to assess intellectual distinction without relying entirely on the vagaries of the fashion of secular intellectual culture. To play the game of prestige, whether in hiring or programming, is to have ceased to have a healthy sense of who one is, and become captive in the circulation of secular tokens whose value is questionable although rarely assessed.

To turn to teaching: while it is not entirely true to say that teachers are born and not made, there is some truth to it, such that departments of Theology in Catholic universities and colleges can limp along in the hope that they get lucky and that their teachers are good enough to avoid a reckoning. During his thirteen years tenure as Chair in the Department of Theology at Notre Dame, John Cavadini made clear that good enough was not good enough. Teaching ability was a major consideration in hiring and continuing assessment of faculty. There were teaching workshops for PhD students who were going to teach one of the core theology courses; assistance was provided regarding syllabi production; and faculty mentorship was ongoing throughout the teaching of the course. Teaching excellence was expected. Among the purposes served was not only the inculcation of literacy in the Christian tradition or traditions, but also the ability to persuade—and not merely insist—that the tradition was not only a source of faith, but a resource to meet the outstanding challenges of our time. John Cavadini would be the first to say that without amazingly committed directors of undergraduate and graduate study, none of this could have been accomplished. Indeed, I suspect that he would give the bulk of the credit to their labors which have borne fruit.

Six years after John Cavadini stepped down as Chair, the Department of Theology at Notre Dame has over four hundred majors and minors in Theology. In times where administrators routinely stress that given the expense of undergraduate education, and students feel pressured to go into majors that have obvious monetary reward, the numbers are a testimony to his legacy in the department.

THE LURE OF BEAUTY

Speaking to all that John Cavadini has accomplished, which has appropriately been recognized in 2018 by the Monika Helwig award for leadership in Catholic education, the insinuation of extraordinary energy that nests both great humility and courage, it is easy to lose the person and especially the well-springs for all the teaching and writing, all the leading, collaboration, programming, thinking, speaking, advising and exhorting. I do not think that this well-spring is easily named, for it is difficult not to think of John Cavadini as being incommunicable in that old-fashioned philosophical sense of not being fully transparent to analysis and substitutable in any fundamental way. Maybe there are many well-springs, perhaps like there are many geysers in Iceland. But the one I want to name is the thirst and lure of beauty.

I think of that thirst as indelibly present as John rode the garbage truck in North Haven (his job in graduate school, as a young husband and father), that is expressed in his love of flowers, which also gets to a deep knowledge, in his love of Dante and Emily Dickenson, as well as in his ecstatic epiphanic poems that marries Dickenson's glaring perception to the rhapsody of the everyday. Expressed above all, however, in his passion for the theological tradition with all its highways and byways, nooks and crannies that satisfies and makes the student want more, and in his conviction that much of it bears on where we are and who we are. He is convinced as few others have been in the past decades that the Catholic theological tradition, and I daresay the Catholic philosophical tradition, as well as the

traditions of liturgy, biblical reflection, and spiritual formation can be relied on as a support to our questions and our being on the way; they can be
regarded as a place where sometimes we get answers, at other times partial
answers, and other times alleviation of our questions through thoughtful
and hopeful recalibration which necessarily leaves questions intact. For, it
remains true for him, that though Christ is the full revelation of the mystery of God, the mystery remains and Christ too is mystery. When it comes
to figures such as Origen and Augustine this passion for the tradition is
truly visceral and elemental.

John Cavadini exercises the magic of bringing us back to Alexandria
in the third century and bringing Alexandria forward into our present. He
exercises the same magic in also bringing us back to Hippo in the fifth
century to the forever searching Augustine who hungers for answers and
finds some. And John Cavidini gives the lie to the belief that Augustine
fails to make it out of the fifth century. Augustine becomes our contemporary, maybe even our future. He does much more than present Augustine's
thought capably and with eloquence; he re-presents Augustine's thinking
such that we share in it and not simply the conclusions. He reads not only
with consummate subtlety and suppleness, but with the deepest love that
can track the smallest of Augustine's intentions and passions. Why? Because
one should, because Augustine can disclose much that is true and fruitful.

But John Cavadini also does it because he can, because he like Augustine is a natural-born teacher. But not only that. In addition, we are drawn
to Augustine's thinking because it is beautiful, sometimes indescribably
so. If a reader can get rid of what covers it over, including her or his own
expectations, then the beauty is revealed. The case of the Church is perhaps
more difficult given all that has marred it over the centuries. Yet Cavadini
is equally reluctant here to withhold. Even if he uses a different vocabulary
he is as prepared as Henri de Lubac and Hans Urs von Balthasar to avow
the splendor of the Church. He is genuinely smitten, and invites us to be.

In this respect, very much like Leo Tolstoy and Fyodor Dostoyevsky,
John Cavadini is committed to the proposition that beauty will save the
world. Like Dostoyevsky, he is convinced that in Christ is the full manifestation of beauty. Like his beloved Augustine he intuits that ultimate beauty
is the triune God whom the Church worships, Catholic universities teach,
both doing so with a view to participation in that which passes understanding and that leads the transformation and elevation of often ugly but ultimately lovely world.

2

Mary's Pondering Heart
and the Idea of a Catholic University

Ann W. Astell

"In polemics against the Church, in the Church's own imagination as expressed
in art and theology, the Catholic Church is uniquely associated with Mary.
Mary remains the person whose name or image will bring
to mind Catholicism most readily."

—John C. Cavadini

On August 26, 2017, Notre Dame President Fr. John Jenkins, CSC,
preached a remarkable homily at an all-university Mass honoring Mary,
Seat of Wisdom. The occasion was celebratory, marking not only the start
of the 2017–2018 academic year, but also the conclusion of the Notre Dame
Trail, a hike of three hundred miles in commemoration of the 175th anniversary of the first arrival in South Bend of Father Edward Sorin, CSC
(1814–1893), the founder of the University, and his companions. The text
of Fr. Jenkins's homily features the Marian character of education at Notre
Dame, the acknowledged flagship for Catholic higher education in the
United States.

In that homily Fr. Jenkins first set the stage for his considerations by alluding to recent violence at the University of Virginia, where "neo-Nazi, anti-Semitic, white supremacist, racist, anti-immigrant and homophobic chants," protests, and counter-protests had "led to violence, injuries, and the death of a young, innocent woman, Heather Heyer."[1] Perhaps recalling the Fighting Irish's own historical battle with the anti-Catholic KKK,[2] Fr. Jenkins saw the "troubled times" of the present as an incentive to reaffirm the Catholic ideal of education. Taking issue with a faculty member at the University of Virginia, who had opined in an article published in *The Chronicle of Higher Education* that "universities exist . . . for epistemic virtues—openness to debate, a commitment to critical inquiry and attention to detail," and are therefore "insufficient for responding" to hatred and violence,[3] Fr. Jenkins described Notre Dame as a Catholic university where the pursuit of truth requires the cultivation not of one but of two, mutually related sets of virtues: "the epistemic virtues of the head and the moral virtues of the heart."[4]

Reminding his audience of Fr. Sorin's ardent Marian devotion, Fr. Jenkins went on to praise Mary, the Mother of God, as the patroness of the University and the Scriptural model who possesses precisely these combined, integrated virtues of head and heart—virtues that flourish through "silent pondering," love, and prayer.[5] He named "the silent, pondering presence of Mary," represented especially in the statues atop the Dome and in the Grotto, "the heart of Notre Dame" and the best guarantee for its educational mission.

As Fr. Jenkins later confided to me, he drew inspiration for this homily from an essay by Fr. Kevin Grove, CSC, on the Mariology of the founder of the Congregation of Holy Cross, Blessed Basil Moreau (1799–1873).

1. I thank Fr. Jenkins for sharing the text of his homily with me. I quote here and in subsequent paragraphs from his unpublished text.

2. See Tucker, *Notre Dame vs. The Klan*.

3. See Chad Wellmon, "For Moral Clarity, Don't Look to Universities." I quote not from Wellmon's article but rather from Fr. Jenkins's summary of it.

4. In accord with the legacy of Blessed Basil Moreau and Fr. Edward Sorin, CSC, education "of heart and mind" is a watchword at Notre Dame. Fr. Joseph Kentenich (1885–1968), the founder of the international Schoenstatt Work, is a kindred spirit in this regard. He emphatically contrasted "organic" and "mechanistic" ways of thinking. "Mechanistic thinking inappropriately separates the mind from the heart," he writes; by contrast, "sound thinking is organic, symbolic, centered, and holistic." See King, *Joseph Kentenich*. See also Peters, *Ecce Educatrix Tua*.

5. For an article on a related theme, see Halpin, "Pondering Heart."

Linking Mary's Immaculate Conception with her suffering at the cross, Fr. Grove explains, "For Moreau, because Mary was created by God to be immaculate and the source of life for the Incarnate Word, she became a co-operator in both the sufferings of her son and in the designs of salvation."[6] Pondering mysteries of inexpressible joy and of unspeakable anguish, Mary—the perfect disciple and helpmate of the Lord, the Mother of God, and "mother to all at the foot of the cross"[7]—can thus teach her children also how to think, how to recognize God's designs, and how to cooperate with love and courage in their fulfillment.

In this essay I want to continue exploring the themes announced by Fr. Jenkins and Fr. Grove by considering more closely the meaning of the Biblical notion of the "thoughts of the heart" in relation to Mary's pure heart, pierced with sorrow. Within this framework, John Cavadini's "Marian Initiative" at the McGrath Institute for Church Life can be seen to resonate strongly with Fr. Jenkins's Marian vision of education at Notre Dame. If Catholic education derives from the Church's own teaching mission, *ex corde ecclesiae*,[8] it also finds its original source in Mary's own heart, *ex corde Mariae*.

THE THOUGHTS OF MARY'S HEART

Fr. Jenkins's homily strongly contrasts Mary's pondering heart and love-filled understanding, on the one hand, with the ideologies that ignited group violence against people and property in Charlottesville, on the other. It argues, moreover, that truer and deeper "thoughts" than these ideologies can be "revealed" in, or "drawn out" of, students and faculty in the university community at Notre Dame through a process of Marian education that participates somehow in the ponderings of Mary's own sinless heart.

This complementary, two-fold view—contrastive and participatory— is anchored in a single Biblical verse with an ambiguous syntax. At the presentation of the Lord in the Temple, forty days after his birth, the mother of Jesus heard the marvelous prophecies of Simeon and Anna concerning her child. Simeon also prophesied, however, concerning Mary herself: "And

6. Grove, "Pondering Heart," 235.

7. Grove, "Pondering Heart," 240.

8. I refer, of course, to Pope John Paul II's Apostolic Constitution on Catholic Universities, "Ex Corde Ecclesiae." Hereafter, I cite from this document parenthetically by paragraph.

thy own soul a sword shall pierce, that the thoughts of many hearts may be revealed" (Luke 2:35).[9] Rendered thus in the 1899 Douay-Rheims translation, the same verse is joined to the preceding one in the New Revised Standard Version, as follows: "This child is destined for the falling and the rising of many in Israel, and to be a sign that will be opposed, so that the inner thoughts of many will be revealed—and a sword will pierce your own soul too" (Luke 2:34–35).

Given the hindsight of history, the meaning of the first part and last part of this prophecy seems clear enough: Jesus and his mother are both destined to suffer. Mary, the Queen of martyrs, will suffer an unspeakable martyrdom; she will stand at the foot of the cross, witness the cruel death of her son, suffer every blow and torment with him. Compassionate with the child of her womb, who is "bone of [her] bone and flesh of [her] flesh" (Gen 2:23),[10] Mary will share in Jesus' Passion and death in an unparalleled way that staggers the imagination. Contemplating the Virgin Mother in her grief, the Church has placed upon her lips the Biblical lament, "Is it nothing to you, all you who pass by? Look and see if there is any sorrow like my sorrow" (Lam 1:12). To symbolize the unsurpassed fullness of Mary's suffering, tradition has indeed multiplied the single sword of Simeon's prophecy to name it a seven-fold sword: "And thy own soul shall be pierced by a sword" seven times: at the prophecy of Simeon, at the flight into Egypt, at the three-day loss of the twelve-year-old, at the meeting on the Via Dolorosa, at Christ's crucifixion, at the taking down of his body, and at its burial.[11]

The moveable phrase "that the thoughts of many hearts may be revealed," however, invites a two-fold interpretation. Taken in its immediate context, the clause might derive its meaning from the prophecy that Mary's child is destined to be "a sign that will be opposed" (Luke 2:34, NRSV). Even when the people followed him after seeing his signs, Jesus in his divine knowledge read their hearts, their secret intentions, and (as the evangelist reports) he "did not trust himself to them, because he knew all men and needed no one to bear witness of man; for he himself knew what was in man" (John 2:24–25, RSV); he knew the thoughts of their hearts.

9. I use here the American edition of the 1899 Douay-Rheims translation. For other translations, see BibleGateway, "Luke 2:35."

10. Unless otherwise indicated, I use the Revised Standard Version, Catholic Edition.

11. In 1239, the founders of the Servites of Mary took up the sorrows of Mary as their special devotion. From 1413, the feast of the Seven Sorrows of the Virgin Mary was observed in Cologne and spread from there. See Rubin, *Mother of God*, 243–55.

Jesus could discern the hidden traps his questioners set for him: 'Why put me to the test, you hypocrites?'" (Matt 22:18). Again and again we read that "the Pharisees and the scribes murmured" against him amongst themselves and to his disciples (Luke 15:2; 19:7; John 6:41) because Jesus scandalized them, eating and drinking with sinners, curing on the Sabbath, forgiving sins, offering his flesh as food; because they envied him his popularity with the people and resented his public criticisms of them. The action taken by Christ's enemies, the crimes with which he was accused, the death-sentence they demanded—all these contradicted him. The denials spoken by Peter, the deal that Judas struck with the elders, the testimony of false witnesses, the rebuke of the high priest, the unjust sentence Pilate passed—all these contradicted him, and in that contradiction of the very Word-made-flesh, "the thoughts of many hearts [were indeed] revealed."

But why does the prophecy also suggest the piercing of Mary's all-human heart as the cause of this revelation? "And thy own soul a sword shall pierce, that the thoughts of many hearts may be revealed" (Luke 2:35, Douay-Rheims).[12] What are the thoughts of Mary's pierced heart and how do they relate to the thoughts of others' hearts? Why is the piercing of her sorrowful heart somehow necessary for the latter's revelation? And what are the human thoughts that have been revealed through Mary's compassion with Christ? Do these thoughts of the heart—Mary's and ours—have anything to do with remembrance, examination, judgment? With education?

Scripture links the pondering of Mary's heart with its sorrowful piercing "that the thoughts of many hearts may be revealed" (Luke 2:35). This mysterious linkage suggests not only that the cruel actions taken against Christ reveal humanity's fallen condition, false judgments, and impious motivations, but also that the piercing of Mary's pure and pondering heart makes possible for humanity a new way of thinking about God and Christ, imparting to Christ's followers a vital knowledge of him (*vitalis Christi cognitio*) that is inseparable from Mary's own death-defying love of him, her faith in him, her hope for him and his saving work.[13] Mary's love does not

12. A survey of the different translations of Luke 2:34–35 reveals that most English translations (including, for example, the American Standard Version, the International Standard Version, and the King James Version) place the clause about the "thoughts of many hearts" at the very end of the second verse, immediately following the prophecy of the piercing of Mary's heart. Some of these, however—for example, the English Standard Version and the Christian Standard Bible—punctuate that Marian prophecy within parentheses or dashes.

13. I echo here Pope Pius X, "Ad Diem Illum Laetissimum," paragraphs 7 and 8,

contradict the Word-made-flesh; her fiat at Nazareth, when repeated at the cross, welcomes the Word's Incarnation anew in the members of his Mystical Body. The piercing of Mary's heart thus entails an entire program for education: "Have this mind among yourselves, which was in Christ Jesus" (Phil 2:5).

An ancient Christian tradition affirms that Mary conceived Christ mentally in faith before she conceived him in her womb: *Fides in mente, Christus in ventre*.[14] Christian art often depicts her at the hour of the Annunciation reading a book that contains the Old Testament prophecies of the Messiah, the royal descendant of David, the great Savior of his people, but also the suffering servant envisioned in Isaiah 53. In the thoughts of her heart, she already understood these prophecies with an unusual clarity and she was mysteriously drawn to them, sensing that they also concerned her somehow. When the angel came to her in Nazareth, she could therefore grasp the import of his message and pronounce her "fiat," her "let it be," her "yes" to God with a humble freedom unmatched in human history. Speaking on behalf of the human race, Mary welcomed the Son of God into the world as "flesh of [her and our] flesh" (cf. Gen 2:23).

Mary rejoiced in God, in his election of her, and in her extraordinary vocation. The philosopher Simone Weil has written that two things are powerful enough to pierce the human heart and to awaken profound thought: the experiences of awe-inspiring beauty and of crushing affliction.[15] The Gospels are exquisite in their portrayal of Mary's heart as prompted to thought by both. In the Magnificat, Mary's hymn of praise spoken in the house of her cousin Elizabeth, Mary voices her thoughts with heart and soul: "My soul magnifies the Lord, and my spirit rejoices in God my Savior, for he has regarded the low estate of his handmaiden" (Luke 1:46–48). Listening to the report of the shepherds describing the glorious song of the angels, Mary "kept all these things, pondering them in her heart" (Luke 2:19).

The verb "to ponder" is linked semantically to the Latin noun "pondus," meaning "weight." It suggests a weighing or evaluation of something upon a scale, but also the intimate knowledge that one gains of something

where the pontiff points to Mary's intimate knowledge of Christ as an enlivening form of cognition that remains essential to Christian life and belief. For discussion of the pedagogical implications, see Peters, *Ecce Educatrix Tua*, 210–11.

14. On this theme in Augustine's writings, see Fitzgerald and Cavadini, "Mary, Mother of God," 554.

15. See Weil, *Waiting for God*, 132, 162.

by carrying it on one's back, at one's waist, or in one's arms. The process of evaluation and decision-making, the weighing of pros and cons, is thus imaged as the shifting of something ponderous from one side to another, as when a mother rocks a baby contemplatively in a cradle or even when one perceives the movement in the womb of an unborn baby.

The picture of grace known as the Mattheiser Madonna (circa 1700), housed in the Basilica of St. Matthias in Trier, Germany, depicts the Mother of Jesus in her pregnancy, tenderly contemplative. Her beautiful face is oval and elegant, her forehead crowned with a radiant halo-diadem. Her dress is a dark blue, almost black—the color of mourning—but richly decorated with embroidered, leafy fronds, teeming with life, in the style of the ornate, dark dresses used to clothe statues of Our Lady of Solitude. (These statues and that title honor Mary in her greatest earthly loneliness on Holy Saturday, during the sorrowful interim after the death of Jesus and before his resurrection.) With that visual cue, the faith-filled "expectancies" of Mary before Christ's birth and before his rising from the tomb are joined together as two mysteries within a single drama of salvation.

The painting's official title "Seat of Wisdom" (*Sedes Sapientiae* in Latin, *Sitz der Weisheit* in German) recalls statues, dating from an earlier period, which show a hieratic Jesus, childlike in size but bearing the facial features of an adult, seated stiffly on Mary's lap as if on a throne of judgment, his hand raised in an expression of divine authority. Whereas the stylized, Romanesque statues of "The Seat of Wisdom" represented Christ as the eternal Logos made flesh and manifested to the world in a human form of a childlike sage, the Mattheiser Madonna shows the Wisdom of God as something hidden in the Virgin's womb, concealed from view. The cloth that covers the Virgin's womb in the painting recalls a Eucharistic veil over a ciborium or chalice.[16] Mary's posture as she leans forward in reverence becomes a figure of meditative thought, contemplating a mystery. The titles of the statues and of the painting are literally identical, but their meaning has shifted, the accent has changed. Incarnate Wisdom is the possessive agent in the former works of art, the One who assumes His seat as a royal throne. Mary is the agent in the latter, the one who contemplates the unseen child within her, to whom she has given a "place" in the double sense of physical implantation and mental attention. Jesus is the content of her maternal thought and, in a certain sense, its embodiment.

16. A similar covering is notable in Jean van Eyck's depiction of a pregnant Mary in the Ghent altarpiece (1430–1432).

The Latin word *sedes* means literally "a seat, a stool, a throne, a chair." It comes from the verb *sedere*, "to sit," which has the extended meanings: "to sit in council, to sit in judgment," "to be inactive, at rest," "to sit with folded hands," "to be settled," "to be firmly determined." The English words *sedition* ("uprising") and *seduction* ("a leading aside") denote violations of civil and domestic order, respectively—a pulling of things out of their proper place *(sedes)*. Connected with the acts of reflection, deliberation, and judgment, and thus with the maintenance of order, the word *sedes* belongs to the classical and medieval vocabulary describing the mind's reception of sensory impressions, its storage of memories in set places *(sedes)* for recall.[17]

The rounded womb upon which the expectant mother rests her gaze symbolizes the outer veil of phenomenal appearances behind which an Other, deeper reality lies. Knowing this Other is, for the pregnant one, a mysterious and veiled knowledge that is inseparable from self-knowledge, since the living self not only contains the Other, but is also connected with it. Mary realized this maternal, sacramental way of thinking in an unsurpassable way, of course, because the child of her womb was God, a mystery greater than any other. Mary's intimate, human knowledge of Christ her Son was inseparable from her faith in him as the Incarnate Word.

The knowing of Mary's pregnancy was also a foreknowing, a prognosis.[18] Christian tradition, meditating upon Mary as the Sorrowful Mother, imagines her holding her baby as "a bag of myrrh that lies between [her] breasts" (Song 1:13)—myrrh being the gift of the Magi foretelling Christ's death (Matt 2:11), the spice mixed with wine and offered to Jesus as he hung on the cross (Mark 15:23), the spice used, together with aloes, to prepare Jesus's body for burial (John 19:39). Christian lyric poetry and carols depict Mary calming her weeping baby with lullabies, even as his cries announce to her his future death.[19] Christian visual art imagines Mary as a

17. On the topic of memorial storage and recall, see Carruthers, *Book of Memory*; Carruthers, *Craft of Thought*.

18. The "kn" of "know" and the "gn" of "pregnant" stem from the same Indo-European root, as do "cognition," "progeny," "generation," "prognosis," "cunning," and "cunt." The two meanings of that root—"to know and to beget"—defy any "partition" because they "continue to entwine through [all] the linguistic changes" (Shipley, *Origins of English Words*, 129). Plato's Diotima teaches in the Symposium that a spiritual pregnancy of thought is innate to men and women alike (see Pender, "Spiritual Pregnancy in Plato's 'Symposium'").

19. See, for example, the lullabies numbered 199 and 202 in Luria and Hoffman, *Middle English Lyrics*.

prophetess who sees in the shadow cast by the outstretched arms of her Son a foreshadowing of his crucifixion. Did not the prophet Simeon tell her, "'Behold, This child is set . . . for a sign that is spoken against (and a sword shall pierce through your own soul also)'" (Luke 2:34–35)?

The evangelist Luke tells us, however, that Mary did not understand the word spoken to her by the twelve-year-old Jesus, who asked his distraught mother, "'How is it that you sought me? Did you not know that I must be in my Father's house?'" (Luke 2:49). The evangelist goes on to repeat the expression that he has used especially to characterize Mary: "His mother kept all these things in her heart" (Luke 2:51). Christ's subsequent growth "in wisdom and in stature" in Nazareth veils Mary's own growth in understanding as she learns from her Son who teaches her, even as he submits himself in obedience to his parents (Luke 2:51–52).

Tradition finds in Mary and Joseph's distressing, three-day search for the boy Jesus a foreshadowing of the three days from Christ's arrest at night on Holy Thursday to his rising from the dead during the Easter Vigil. The Church's meditation finds a Paschal preparation in this earlier search and Mary's pondering over it, a schooling for heart and mind that prepared Mary to endure with an invincible faith the agony of Christ's Passion and death. The Gospel according to Saint John describes the *altera Maria*, Mary Magdalene, searching tearfully for Christ's body in the garden and encountering the risen Lord there (John 20:1–19), but the Scriptures do not record that Christ's mother searched then for her Son. The implication is that Mary somehow already knew; she had no need to search. The same faith with which she welcomed the Incarnation greeted Jesus at his rising. Perhaps her Son repeated at Easter the words once spoken by Elizabeth in his mother's praise: "'Blessed is she who believed that there would be a fulfillment of what was spoken to her from the Lord'" (Luke 1:45).

Mary's pondering heart, schooled in the Scriptures and by her Son's intimate instruction, understood what even Jesus' closest other disciples had failed to understand. "'O foolish men, and slow of heart to believe all that the prophets have spoken! [Jesus tells the disciples on the road to Emmaus] Was it not necessary that the Christ should suffer these things and enter into his glory?'" (Luke 24:25). When the evangelist records that the "hearts" of these same disciples were "burning within [them]" as the risen Jesus instructed them that day (cf. Luke 24:32), he returns us to the prophecy of Simeon with which we began: "And thy own soul a sword shall pierce, that the thoughts of many hearts may be revealed" (Luke 2:35, Douay-Rheims).

EX CORDE MARIAE: CATHOLIC EDUCATION AND
MARIAN INITIATIVE AT NOTRE DAME

Saint Pope John Paul II's Apostolic Constitution on Catholic Universities, *Ex corde ecclesiae,* does not mention Mary explicitly, but it was solemnly promulgated on August 15, 1990, the Feast of the Assumption of the Blessed Virgin Mary. This is no mere coincidence. A Marian template clearly informs the Apostolic Constitution in at least three ways: in its incarnational formulation of the idea of the Catholic university; in its characterization of the integrative mode of research appropriate to the Catholic university; and in its description of the mission of service of the Catholic university.

Citing Blessed John Henry Cardinal Newman's *The Idea of a University* (1854), John Paul II emphasizes that the search for truth—a search intrinsic to the dignity of the human person—unites every academic field. Especially consecrated to the "cause of truth," the Catholic university sees "the research of all aspects of truth in their connection with the supreme Truth."[20] This common, transcendental goal has the power to form the university as a whole—its administrators, faculty, students, staff—into a community of persons, "*a 'living union' of individual organisms* dedicated to the search for truth."[21]

This "'living union' of individual organisms" (a phrase so evocative of Mary's spiritual and physical two-in-oneness with Christ and of the Church herself as Christ's Mystical Body) is meant to be fruitful, according to the pontiff, in human "culture," which he terms "the highest and incarnate expression" of Christ's liberation in Truth of "every human reality."[22] The Catholic university should facilitate the Church's "dialogue with people of every culture" and the "*incarnation* of the richness of the salvific message" in every culture and field of human activity."[23]

Given this goal, John Paul II insists, "In a Catholic university, research necessarily includes (a) the search for an *integration of knowledge,* (b) a dialogue between faith and reason, (c) an ethical concern, and (d) a theological perspective."[24] The discovery of data cannot be an end in itself, but requires

20. John Paul II, "Ex Corde Ecclesiae," par. 4.

21. John Paul II, "Ex Corde Ecclesiae," par. 6.

22. John Paul II, "Ex Corde Ecclesiae," s.v. conclusion.

23. John Paul II, "Ex Corde Ecclesiae," par. 16, emphasis added. In footnote 16, John Paul II explains that he uses the term "culture" in both a "humanistic" and a "socio-historical" sense.

24. John Paul II, "Ex Corde Ecclesiae," par. 15.

a further quest for meaning that opens on to "moral, spiritual, and religious dimensions."[25] (We have seen this integration of knowledge as a hallmark of Mary's sapiential, maternal thought, the "pondering" of her heart.)

Finally, the pontiff instructs, the moral and religious dimensions of study and research at a Catholic university necessarily oblige the members of the university to a four-fold mission of service: to Church and society, in pastoral ministry, through cultural dialogue, and evangelization. For all of these, Mary, the Christ-bearer, is an indispensable model and motherly intercessor.

The singular status of Mary as archetype and Mother of the Church inspired John Cavadini, director of the McGrath Institute for Church Life (hereafter MICL) to launch a Marian Initiative at the University of Notre Dame in 2013, which had been proclaimed a "Year of Faith" by Pope Benedict XVI. For Cavadini, as for Fr. Jenkins in the historic 2017 homily described at the start of this essay, Mary's pondering heart is the "heart of Notre Dame" as a Catholic university and the best protection for its Catholic identity and educational mission.

The stated premise of the MICL Marian Initiative indirectly alludes to *Ex corde ecclesiae* when it points to Mary, the God-bearer, as the one who imparts an "intimate truth"[26] and who witnesses in a unique way to Incarnate Truth. Echoing John Paul II's language of incarnation and culture, Cavadini writes: "Devotion to Mary is devotion to the Incarnation, the central mystery of the Christian faith." A historical person, Mary preserves the personhood of her Son as a palpable reality, imparting a vital knowledge of him that is inseparable from love and irreducible to mere information. "Mary places us in the concrete," Cavadini observes, and thus induces an application and holistic integration of speculative knowledge, of abstract concepts, and of creedal formulations. Mary is, moreover, "the most inculturated person in the Church," who has been "warmly received into the imaginations of Christians of all cultures," inspiring works of art, customs, institutions, and charitable works worldwide.

Remembering that "Fr. Sorin's founding of Notre Dame is steeped in a Marian vision" that "integrate[s] openness to learning" within a life dedicated to "action and contemplation," Cavadini seeks to recover and renew this vision as a source of flourishing for the University, whose very name

25. John Paul II, "Ex Corde Ecclesiae," par. 7.

26. In discussing the Marian Initiative, I quote from an unpublished text, kindly shared with me by John Cavadini.

identifies it as a "school of Mary." The statue of Mary already overlooks the University from her perch atop the Dome and, in another guise, she welcomes her children in the Lourdes Grotto, the "cave of candles," on campus.[27] If Mary herself becomes even more palpably present at Notre Dame in the faculty, among the students, in the subject matter of courses, in research topics, in volunteer service projects, and in the liturgy, Cavadini argues, Christ himself will be more vitally present, and the University will secure and strengthen its Catholic identity.

As director of the MICL, Cavadini desires to spur Marian scholarship and service at Notre Dame and beyond through programming at the institute. Although the Marian Initiative has not yet been endowed, Cavadini has already employed some of the MICL's resources toward that end.

As part of the MICL's Marian initiative and to mark its launch, for example, Cavadini hosted a major conference entitled "Mary on the Eve of the Second Vatican Council," October 6–8, 2013, at which fifteen scholars presented papers on aspects of pre-conciliar Marian teaching and devotion that might be resources for the Church today, fifty years later. The collected essays in the 2017 volume co-edited by John Cavadini and Danielle Peters have brought the rich fruit of that conference to a large, academic readership.[28] Through Cavadini's efforts, the University of Notre Dame Press in 2017 also republished in paperback a now classic 1958 collection edited by Edward D. O'Connor, CSC, *The Dogma of the Immaculate Conception: History and Significance*, making it available for classroom use.[29]

This sort of theological research and reflection stands as one pillar of the three-fold Marian Initiative already undertaken by Cavadini and his colleagues at the MICL. A second pillar seeks to combine "mind" with "heart" through Marian coursework and research opportunities for undergraduates. Responding to a student's interest, Leonard DeLorenzo offered an MICL internship to Colleen Halpin, whose research on the Mariologies of Edward Sorin and Basil Moreau, CSC, was published online in the *Church Life Journal* (October 7, 2017) in an article entitled "The Pondering Heart: Notre Dame's Special Consecration to Our Lady." This essay launched a yearlong project that, on the one hand, was dedicated to studying the Marian devotions of particular saints (e.g., Thérèse of Lisieux,

---

27. See Corson, *Cave of Candles*.

28. Cavadini and Peters, *Mary on the Eve of the Second Vatican Council*.

29. O'Connor, *Dogma of the Immaculate Conception*.

Teresa of Calcutta, Maximillian Kolbe) and, on the other, highlighted the Marian devotions of current Notre Dame students.

Supplementing regularly offered undergraduate Theology classes on Marian topics—for example, Maxwell Johnson's "Mary and the Saints," Timothy Matovina's course on Our Lady of Guadelupe, Ann Astell's "Immaculate Conception" class, and Brian Daley's course on "Mary"—the MICL, in collaboration with the Department of Theology, has recently offered one-credit "Know Your Catholic Faith" classes on "Mary in the Movies" (taught by Danielle Peters) and "Fatima (1917–2017): History, Devotion, and Theology" (co-taught by Ann Astell and John Cavadini). As part of the "Mary in the Movies" class, the MICL offered two public lectures and a well-attended screening of the 2015 film *Full of Grace,* written and directed by Andrew Hyatt and produced by Terence Berden.

A third pillar of Cavadini's Marian Initiative at the MICL is the thoughtful, beautiful renewal of traditional Marian devotions. Every October, for example, the MICL, especially through the work of Jessica Keating, leads a "Rosary for Life" in the Basilica of the Sacred Heart, using hymns and meditations that match the different mysteries of the rosary and that highlight their thematic relevance to the dignity of human life. Beginning in 2015, initially through the efforts of Danielle Peters, the MICL has sponsored an annual Advent pilgrimage, welcoming "town and gown" participants to view a campus-wide exhibit of international Christmas crèches, on loan from the International Marian Research Institute at the University of Dayton, which vividly demonstrate a Marian, Incarnational inculturation. In May, 2016, through the talents of Carolyn Pirtle, the MICL launched its renewal of the annual May crowning of a statue of the Virgin Mary, which is carried in procession across campus from the Lourdes Grotto to the Chapel of Our Lady of Mercy in Geddes Hall, the pilgrims' walk accompanied by the joyful singing of litanies and the sprinkling of rose petals.

These already accomplished ventures in Marian scholarship, pedagogy, and devotional practice are few in comparison to the many that Cavadini hopes to actualize. In collaboration with Timothy O'Malley and the Notre Dame Center for Liturgy, for example, he envisions a series of workshops for priests, to reinvigorate preaching on Marian themes and dogmas. He seeks to establish institutional ties and opportunities for regular scholarly exchanges with the International Marian Research Institute and the Marian Library at the University of Dayton. He wants the MICL to see to it that pilgrimages are regularly offered, in collaboration with the Office of

Campus Ministry, to Marian pilgrimages places in the United States and abroad (Lourdes, Guadalupe, Fatima).

For John Cavadini, these and other good works, realized in family-like collaboration with others, are like flowers in a spiritual bouquet offered to our Lady. I have sometimes caught him in the early morning in the sacristy, quietly arranging in a vase the flowers he—often accompanied by his wife Nancy—brings weekly to place before the statue of our Lady in the "Seat of Wisdom" chapel in Malloy Hall. These flowers wordlessly bespeak his love for our Lady and make the niche where her statue stands come alive with color and fragrance. Because of the presence of these flowers, anonymously presented in the early morning or on the weekend, the students, faculty, and staff who enter the chapel to pray in the course of the week more easily find themselves in a place where Mary's presence is felt, together with Christ's in the tabernacle. Offered to her with devotion, these flowers too—and the deeds and petitions they represent—become objects of Mary's pondering heart, given to God.[30]

30. I want to express my personal gratitude to John Cavadini, through whom, as chair of the Department of Theology, I came to Notre Dame in 2007. I gave an earlier version of part of this essay at the 2018 Edith Stein Conference at Notre Dame, which was co-organized by Katherine Smith and Molly Weiner, whom I also wish to thank.

3

The Pursuit and Remembrance of Excellence in University Culture

Leonard J. DeLorenzo

"We become what we love and who we love shapes what we become."

—St. Clare of Assisi

THE PURSUIT OF EXCELLENCE

Universities love excellence. Within their classrooms and laboratories, publications and departments, these institutions spur their students to desire excellence, expect their faculty to project excellence, and prod their alumni to fund excellence. If St. Clare is right in saying that we become what we love, then the habitual pursuit of excellence should breed excellence in these institutions and those who abide within them.

No institution would claim to love mediocrity or zealously promote the status quo; rather, the shared vernacular of modern universities is to aim for unique contributions to the wellbeing of society, to make groundbreaking discoveries in the name of progress, and to educate students to make an impact on the world.[1] These aspirations are common to institutions of higher education. To say, therefore, that such institutions love excellence is not to say anything very interesting.

What is interesting is to consider exactly what each considers "well-being" to be, how each measures "progress," and which kinds of "impact" count. They all pursue excellence, but excellence itself is not a thing, person, or definite end. Excellence has to do with a quality of commitment where the really decisive thing comes in response to the question, "Commitment to what or to whom?"

Clare of Assisi, who never taught at, administered, funded, or even stepped foot in an institution of higher education, grasped this perfectly. Her vision is the vision of a saint, for whom, following the words quoted above, her wisdom is expressed as follows:

> If we love things, we become a thing. If we love nothing, we become nothing. Imitation is not a literal mimicking of Christ, rather it means becoming the image of the beloved, an image disclosed through transformation. This means we are to become vessels of God's compassionate love for others.

We become what we love not in terms of strict reduplication, but rather in terms of being shaped to a certain pattern and way of being. Who or what we take as worthy of imitation forms not only what we become capable of, but what kind of persons we become.

The "good" that institutions of higher education seek is ultimately the most important thing about these places. This understanding of the "good" goes beyond what is stated; it is captured more in what is practically

---

1. A quick perusal of the mission statements of top-tier universities (or really any-tier university) supports this claim. For example, Harvard College's mission statement reads: "The mission of Harvard College is to educate the citizens and citizen-leaders for our society. We do this through our commitment to the transformative power of a liberal arts and sciences education . . . From this, we hope that students will begin to fashion their lives by gaining a sense of what they want to do with their gifts and talents, assessing their values and interests, and learning how they can best serve the world." Duke's reads: "Duke University seeks to engage the mind, elevate the spirit, and stimulate the best effort of all who are associated with the University; to contribute in diverse ways to the local community, the state, the nation and the world; and to attain and maintain a place of real leadership in all that we do." While Claremont McKenna College's states that: "Its mission, within the mutually supportive framework of The Claremont Colleges, is to educate its students for thoughtful and productive lives and responsible leadership in business, government, and the professions, and to support faculty and student scholarship that contribute to intellectual vitality and the understanding of public policy issues."

pursued and how. These institutions provide not just access to things to think about, or resources for doing this thinking, but even more they create cultures for how to think, how to desire, and how to evaluate success and failure. The kinds of habits that are recommended and the regular practices that are promoted are informed by the particular commitments these institutions make, whether those commitments are explicitly stated or implicitly operative.

Among the many other initiatives John Cavadini has launched over the years, one in particular provides a view on what "good" a Catholic university is called to pursue and what lives given over to that good might look like. This is an initiative in which the possibilities for human flourishing takes the widest possible horizon. It was created at the boundary of the academy, where specialists and laypersons, students and curious seekers could meet together to be nourished by the fruits of scholarship and spirituality alike. This initiative bears the title "Saturdays with the Saints," which Cavadini founded in 2010, hosting lectures every Saturday of a home football game at Notre Dame to uplift the witness of different saints. Though offered as a gift to visitors to campus and the local community, with videos made available for free to anyone online afterwards, this series has also become a witness to the meaning and possibilities of Catholic higher education.

From the mission statement of the University of Notre Dame, we read:

> The University prides itself on being an environment of teaching and learning that fosters the development in its students of those disciplined habits of mind, body, and spirit that characterize educated, skilled, and free human beings. In addition, the University seeks to cultivate in its students not only an appreciation for the great achievements of human beings but also a disciplined sensibility to the poverty, injustice and oppression that burden the lives of so many. The aim is to create a sense of human solidarity and concern for the common good that will bear fruit as learning becomes service to justice.[2]

This initiative's popular but scholarly study of the saints draws attention to how each saint and all of them together, in and through their words and deeds, create the conditions of human solidarity and dedicate themselves to the concern not for their own private gain but in fact for the common good. They commit themselves to Jesus Christ whom they love, and by the power of the one they love, they are transformed into free human

2. University of Notre Dame, "Mission Statement."

beings who give themselves over to the healing of poverty, injustice, and oppression. The basis of this transformation is always a set of disciplined habits of mind, body and spirit that foster a holy and loving character in which what the saints do and teach are true expressions of who they have become. On Saturday mornings several hours before kickoff in a space where the university and the world meet, the "good" that a Catholic institution of higher education pursues and for which it seeks to form its students is made evident in the witness of the saints, who are alternately scholars, innovators, reformers, preachers, teachers, healers, parents, confessors, and visionaries. As Cavadini is fond of saying at the beginning of each lecture, "The saints are bearers of light in a world that sometimes seems to be filled with darkness." They testify to what is good, true, and beautiful, and therefore worthy of pursuit.

With this twin backdrop of higher education's love of excellence and the witness of the saints as a statement to the end by which excellence is to be measured, I will lay out the remainder of this essay in three principal parts. First, I will turn to John Henry Newman's *Idea of a University* to elucidate the aim of education itself, especially in a university setting. Second, I will diagnose how universities themselves fall prey to and perpetuate the "trap of excellence," when the pursuit of presumed excellence becomes uncoupled from the remembrance of the true ends of excellence. Third, I will attend to the necessary reunion of the pursuit and remembrance of excellence through its proper expression as virtue. In the second and third sections, John Cavadini's own vision and thought will guide the inquiry, specifically though not exclusively from one of his own Saturdays with the Saints lectures, on Saint Augustine as Saint of Suspicion.[3]

MORE THAN IDEAS

John Henry Newman's *Idea of a University* is at once a treatise on how and why to educate young people in the liberal arts and sciences, and a proposal about the theory of the university itself. In fact, the image of the university becomes, as it were, a model for the formation of the student's intellectual cultivation, while the proper cultivation of each student redounds to the wholeness and health of the institution itself. In Newman's vision, neither the university nor a student's mind are mere storehouses of resources or

3. The text of this lecture is available at Cavadini, "Augustine," plus an accompanying video of the lecture from McGrathND, "Augustine."

data; rather, Newman beholds an image of wholeness for each, where the nourishment of a kind of culture in the former and of a kind of character in the latter is the true aim.

As Newman writes in the preface of his work,

> Certainly a liberal education does manifest itself in a courtesy, propriety, and polish of word and action, which is beautiful in itself, and acceptable in others; but it does much more. It brings the mind into form,—for the mind is like the body. Boys outgrow their shape and their strength; their limbs have to be knit together, and their constitution needs tone. Mistaking animal spirits for vigour, and overconfident in their health, ignorant of what they can bear and how to manage themselves, they are immoderate and extravagant; and fall into sharp sicknesses. This is an emblem of their minds; at first they have no principles laid down within them as a foundation for the intellect to build upon; they have no discriminating convictions, and no grasp of consequences. And therefore they talk at random, if they talk much, and cannot help being flippant, or what is emphatically called "*young.*" They are merely dazzled by phenomena, instead of perceiving things as they are.[4]

Guiding students to know various or even a great many things as mere data is not the true end of education. Instead, the cultivation of the mind—indeed, of the whole person—to wield knowledge responsibly, to make discriminating judgments, to grasp consequences, and to develop towards a "connected view or grasp of things" is the aim.[5] None of these operations are reducible to any of the data that may enter into the mind; they are marks of the mind itself at work, for which holistic cultivation is necessary. Though one might conceive of various departments of the mind that concern themselves with disparate facts in isolation from one another, Newman counters that,

> All that exists, as contemplated by the human mind, forms one large system or complex fact, and this of course resolves itself into an indefinite number of particular facts which, as being portions

---

4. Newman, *Idea of a University*, xlii–xliii. Or, as Josef Pieper might put it, quite succinctly, following St. Thomas Aquinas, the "young" are not yet but must become appropriately "prudent," and prudence, as a virtue, is a perfected ability that requires cultivation (see Pieper, *Four Cardinal Virtues*, 3–42).

5. Newman, *Idea of a University*, xliii. There is of course a strong resemblance in Newman's thought here to Augustine's in Book X of his *Confessions*.

of a whole, have countless relations of every kind one towards another. Knowledge is the apprehension of these facts, whether in themselves, or in their mutual positions and bearings. And, as all taken together form one integral subject for contemplation, so there are no natural or real limits between part and part; one is ever running into another; all, as viewed by the mind, are combined together, and possess a correlative character one with another.[6]

The primary concern for education is not coterminous with the ends of each separate discipline but rather transcends all of them and incorporates each of them. The point is the training and disciplining of the mind itself, for how it becomes capable of holding types of knowledge, what it does with this knowledge, and the fruits that grow therefrom. This moves beyond the rational faculties of the mind as if the mind existed in isolation; indeed, this is a matter of the cultivation of the will and of the affections alongside the maturation of the mind. The dispositions of a person and the decisions he or she makes call upon the concerted action of the mind, the will, and the heart.[7]

It is therefore the shape of the whole educational enterprise at a university that matters to the cultivation of students. Newman argues that vague or partial views that inform the aims of an institution are comparatively less effective in shaping and forming those who partake in its educational culture than more complete views operating in the culture, even if those views are erroneous and inadequate to the demands of reality. Consistency of intellectual enterprise—even when that consistency is founded upon fallacious assumptions—is where the true power of education lives.[8]

It is therefore the ultimate, operative commitment of the institution as a whole that is of incomparable importance to the education of its students and its service to society. By its very nature, a *university* is (or ought to be) committed not just to studying the great number of things that exist, but indeed the wholeness of all that exists. Each discipline does not provide its own end within itself, nor do the ends of education come from the majority agreement of the respective departments. The pursuit of excellence

---

6. Newman, *Idea of a University*, 33–34.

7. Parity exists with the vision of Christian Education espoused by Basil Moreau, founder of the Congregation of Holy Cross. See especially Moreau, "Christian Education," 329–76; "Circular Letter 36," 415–23.

8. See Newman, *Idea of a University*, xliv.

in higher education rises up to the heights of "how" all things relate and ultimately to the question of "why."[9]

The university itself is to be the institutional image of the cultivated mind, where, again, "there are no natural or real limits between part and part; one is ever running into another . . . possess[ing] a correlative character one with another." The disciplines within a university are always necessarily parts of a whole. Here is the basis of Newman's theory of the integration of the disciplines, held within the consistent and comprehensive intellectual enterprise of the university.[10]

So what is the basis and goal of the entire enterprise of a particular university? This is the key question, for its ultimate aim will inform all its constituent endeavors. No matter how seemingly dignified or praiseworthy a stated aim might be—whether for the more just ordering of society or the spread of prosperity or the perpetual renewal of industry—any measurement of a university according to utility diminishes the mission of the university itself. By the logic of utility, all operations of a university and therefore all growth in its students are eventually rendered to the scale that the preferred type of utility provides.

Newman opposes Locke on this point, accusing Locke of valuing education *only* according to what will be useful to a student's future profession or trade, with a tone that condemns any teaching that tends towards the general cultivation of the mind itself.[11] Going beyond Locke but with the same logic, another utilitarian view may be espoused whereby the furthering of a particular field or discipline becomes the point of education—all this does is replace the student with the field of study in the calculus of utility.[12] If the cultivation of the mind is a good in itself, as Newman contends, then the mission of a university must, in the end, be the pursuit of truth itself.[13]

9. See, for example, Newman, *Idea of a University*, 38.

10. For an elucidation of theology's crucial place within the university, see Cyril O'Regan's essay in the present volume.

11. Newman, *Idea of a University*, 120–21.

12. Newman, *Idea of a University*, 121–22.

13. As John Cavadini has pointed out over and over again, the mission statement of the University of Notre Dame explicitly states that: "The University is dedicated to the pursuit and sharing of truth for its own sake." This means, of course, that the ultimate measure of the university's success—its excellence—is not to be rendered according to any utilitarian ends. See University of Notre Dame, "Mission Statement."

Rightly conceived, excellence for a university is measured according to the study of *what is* in all its dimensions including considerations for the universe's rationality, origin, and final destiny. Secondarily and only secondarily is a university to be measured according to the value of economic ends, civic ends, etc. Bringing his argument together, Newman contends that we must, "take 'useful' to mean, not what is simply good, but what *tends* to good, or is the *instrument* of good. . . . The useful is not always good, the good is always useful. Good is not only good, but reproductive of good."[14] As the success of the student is ultimately measured according to the enrichment of the quality of the mind itself and the cultivation of character, so the success of the university is ultimately measured according to its free and uninhibited pursuit and contemplation of truth for its own sake, as a mission embedded within the culture of the institution. Excellence, for an institution of higher education, is in the quality of the commitment to this mission.

When a university serves only a technocratic paradigm, it loses its intrinsic value while it becomes subservient to the mechanisms of commerce and industry. When an institution subscribes to that paradigm, that becomes the formative mold for those educated therein. Ironically, in the name of liberty and progress, the whole educational project becomes a clandestine form of servitude as students and faculty alike become restricted to the modes of ascent prescribed by the dominant culture.[15] In truth, a healthy society needs more from its citizens than technical proficiency and aptitude for the various professions, especially as dictated by the market. It needs persons who, again, wield knowledge responsibly, make discriminating judgments, grasp consequences, and develop towards a connected view or grasp of things. These are marks of true freedom. As such, Nemwan concludes his warning against reducing the value of education to utilitarian measures by arguing that, "while [a person 'educated' for utilitarian purposes alone] thus contributes more effectually to the accumulation of national wealth he becomes himself more and more degraded as a rational being. In proportion as his sphere of action is narrowed his mental powers and habits become contracted; and he resembles a subordinate part of some powerful machinery, useful in its place, but insignificant and worthless out of it."[16]

14. Newman, *Idea of a University*, 124.

15. For a sustained argument on this point, see especially Deneen, *Why Liberalism Failed*, s.v. chapter 4 and chapter 5.

16. Newman, *Idea of a University*, 127.

On this final point, Newman carries forward the wisdom of one of his own patron saints and models of education, St. Philip Neri. To a young man, Francesco Zazzara, who had set his heart on worldly ascent and rendered his own education and growth only according to the stations of life he might later come to accompany in the paradigm that the dominant culture of his day provided, Neri said:

> "O happy you! Now you are studying; after a time you will be made a doctor and begin to gain money, and to advance your family; you will become an advocate, and then some day you may be raised to be a prelate," and so he went on describing step by step all the honors which the world could give, or which had ever passed through the youth's imagination, repeating again: "O happy you! Then you will be looking for nothing more." Francesco thought that the Saint meant what he said; but at last Philip pressing the youth's head to his bosom, whispered in his ear, "And then?"[17]

This young man seemed to be pursuing excellence, but what Neri like Newman after him discerned is that something else is going on here: ambition is masquerading as excellence.

THE TRAP OF EXCELLENCE

The desire to be acclaimed as excellent is the undoing of excellence. This desire begins with subtle roots but spreads voraciously. It feels good to be lauded, especially when the praise has been earned in some way. The elation of discovery or the joy of creation brings satisfaction in itself, but when this satisfaction is joined by the additional satisfaction of others recognizing the accomplishment and celebrating *you* for being the one to do it, the delight grows. But what about those times when the accomplishment is great but the praise you receive is minimal, or vice versa? Which is preferred? Most would claim the former but actually prefer the latter. The desire to be praised seems to outpace the desire to actually be praiseworthy, not to mention the desire to praise someone else. Over time, in the heart of the individual and in the halls of the academy, the operative but unannounced motivation becomes the desire to be praised—i.e., to be *called* "excellent."

In Book I of his *Confessions*, St. Augustine diagnoses the whole course of his education as tutoring him to fan the flames of this hidden desire above all:

17. Bacci, *Life of St. Philip Neri*, 270–71; Robinson, *In No Strange Land*, 120.

> I hankered to win glory in our contests, and to have my ears tick-
> led by tall stories which only made them itch more hotly, and all
> the while that same curiosity more and more inflamed my eyes
> with lust for the public shows which are the games of grown-ups.
> The people who provide these entertainments enjoy such celeb-
> rity and public esteem that nearly all of them hope their children
> will follow their example (I.10.16). . . . Even in this troth-breaking
> the approval of people all around me rang in my ears: "Fine! Well
> done!" To pander to this world is to fornicate against you [O God],
> but so loudly do they shout, "Well done!" that one feels ashamed to
> fall short of their expectations (I.21). . . . I was myself dominated
> by a vain urge to excel. . . . These same sins grow worse as we grow
> older (I.19.30).[18]

In all the things he learned in his liberal arts education—from history and literature to philosophy and rhetoric, Augustine comes to see that
the primary and ultimate education was actually an education in desiring
praise for oneself. The pursuit of excellence has become the relentless pursuit of being called "excellent."

In his 2015 Saturdays with the Saints lecture on "Augustine: Saint of
Suspicion," John Cavadini channeled Augustine's own critique of himself
and the culture of education in which he was reared towards ultimately the
"meaning of life" but more proximately to the culture of modern universities. As Cavadini writes,

> I am suggesting that Augustine's idea of original sin—pride or
> *superbia*—is the primal hermeneutic of suspicion, which, when
> applied to cultural realities, unmasks their pretensions and reveals
> the deepest source of social stagnation and human decline in the
> refusal of humility, understood as a passion for gratitude for our
> own being as a gift; that is, a refusal to praise God. Under the rubric
> of "the pursuit of excellence," or, in Latin, sometimes "*excellentia*"
> but more often "*virtus*"—so often heard in political speeches and
> not least at universities—is disguised the very thing that causes
> human communities to come apart. It's not that there is no true
> excellence or virtue to pursue; that would be outright nihilism.
> Rather, it's that the pursuit of excellence by fallen human beings
> inevitably tilts towards the rejection of excellence or virtue, even
> in its very pursuit, because the pursuit of excellence is inevitably

---

18. Augustine, *Confessions*.

confused with the pursuit of praise, glory, fame, or, we could say, translating into our own idiom, prestige.[19]

This Augustinian critique requires me to change the first line of this essay. Rather than saying, "universities love excellence," Cavadini's Augustinian reading reveals that "universities lust after prestige." And yet, something even deeper than a mere substitution of ends has taken place: to wit, the substitution is also an act of counterfeit. The covetousness of lust pretends to be the generosity of love, while the hankering for prestige in a thoroughgoing pedagogy of self-promotion passes for excellence according to the pursuit of truth. The upshot is a culture that forms people to delight in recognition—being praised—more than and perhaps even in place of delighting in the cultivation of the mind, the development of character, and the collaborative enterprise of contemplating the breadth and depth of *what is*.

Connecting back to that *other* Augustinian—John Henry Newman— what Cavadini argues is that the deepest sickness in modern universities is not found in fragmentary or partial agendas, but rather more often, in the furtive (or not so furtive) agendas that are, in the final analysis, completely ordered by the lust for prestige. What matters is not merely what is taught or studied, or what is published or promoted, but rather how thinking is done, how success is measured, and how merit is evaluated. Students are taught to desire according to the rubrics of prestige, as faculty are expected to research and publish by its rules, while alumni are encouraged to boast of and donate to their alma mater on the basis of the perceived or potential superiority of this institution relative to its peers. Rather than a cooperative endeavor wherein one might even and indeed must rejoice at *another*'s success as much as if not more than one's own, the pursuit of "truth" becomes a competition. No longer is the point to ascend together towards truth, to contemplate it more fully and honestly, but rather to be seen as the one who has contributed the most.

The choice here is not between progress and stagnation, ambition and laziness, excellence and mediocrity, though that is what the pedagogy of prestige forms one to believe. The fundamental choice is about how to measure "success" or "growth" or "excellence"—that is to say, by which standard or end. It is a question about mission.

By the pedagogy of prestige, "excellence" tends to be ordered to rankings, status, marketability, reputation, or, in language familiar to Augustine,

19. Cavadini, "Augustine."

"worldly praise." By contrast, in the pedagogy of gratitude that Cavadini is recalling from Augustine that is at once a personal and communal endeavor to rejoice in truth, "excellence" is inseparable from "virtue." In the former pedagogy, the kind of mastery that matters concerns learning how to elicit esteem and admiration from others, while in the latter, mastery has to do with the cultivation of the person who might participate responsibly, discerningly, and indeed creatively in the community of which he or she is a part.

The quality of mind and the training of the will and affections that Newman reveres as the true purpose of a university education is one in which training and habituation—over a long course of study, touching on the whole of the person and duly concerned with the operation of his mind—forms a kind of character.[20] In a culture, however, where the overriding lesson is not in how to acquire virtue but rather how to boast of it—including and especially when the boasting is virtually undetectable—then another kind of character is formed, one that bears the marks of an addiction to *being praised*. This is the most severe form of vulnerability and insecurity, because this makes one subservient to whatever the dominant culture happens to find fitting for approval.

Cavadini comments on the corrosiveness of this prideful lust for prestige, before beginning to suggest what the antidote to this sickness would be in the witness of the saints. I quote him here at length:

> To claim one's virtue as ultimately one's own, to claim that one's excellence is not ultimately a gift of God's grace rather than a merit, deserving of praise, is to situate oneself, even offer oneself, as entirely assimilable to whatever the power structure has decided is meaningful, praiseworthy, and glorious. But if there is no place within the self which is ultimately thought of as praiseworthy, if one's virtue—what is absolutely best and excellent in oneself—is a gift and not a heroic achievement in the first instance, then there is no place in oneself for the power structure to "catch" in one's soul, no place for the co-optation of excellence into (in Augustine's terms) empire. A whole new realm, previously out of the reach of the imagination, becomes revealed as the martyr's resistance to prevailing opinion to the point of death becomes testimony to their own courage as a gift of God, and to their own gratitude for the gift of Christ's sacrifice, to which they bear witness. These

---

20. For a classic Aristotelian account of "excellence," see Durant, *Story of Philosophy*, 76, quoting from *Nichomachean Ethics* (i.7, ii.4).

47

stories are "lights," they move us to see an excellence which is not bound to the vocabulary of power and prestige, one that tells of the glory of the Creator, and all that he has created, not the glory of the structure of power. Finally, human excellence, in the voice and witness of the martyrs, is allowed to speak in a language that rises above the vocabulary of power and prestige as supposedly absolute. And if the human virtue or excellence of the martyrs now stands as testimony to the glory of God, then they cast in a new light everything they presuppose—i.e., "nature"—the very existence of the one who is virtuous and that of every other human being. Nature, in the light of grace, recovers the sheen of wonder.[21]

Education according to this understanding of "excellence" as "virtue" returns the world to learners as something to be pondered rather than used for one's own purposes. This is the condition of the possibility of true freedom of speech.

THE REMEMBRANCE OF EXCELLENCE

When Newman claims that "a liberal education . . . brings the mind into form," he notes how principles are laid down and the powers of discernment are developed so that the "*young*" learn to stop being "merely dazzled by phenomena" and instead begin to "perceive things as they are."[22] When that education inculcates the lust for prestige, however, the form that the mind takes is one that is perpetually trapped by the dazzling phenomena of the ephemeral appearances of "worldly praise." Rather than being opened to the world and to others, the ones schooled in the ways of praise-seeking are locked up within themselves. This is precisely that from which the "liberal education" is meant offer liberation: being closed up in one's own private world. This education ought to heal one of the lust for prestige.[23]

But how can this form of healing through education come about if the institutions that are supposed to tutor students towards this freedom are themselves stuck in the rut of chasing after prestige? In response,

---

21. Cavadini, "Augustine."

22. See again Newman, *Idea of a University*, xlii–xliii.

23. As the *Catechism of the Catholic Church* (§407) states: "Ignorance of the fact that man has a wounded nature inclined to evil gives rise to serious errors in the areas of education, politics, social action, and morals." Cavadini cites this line in the paper "Lights Along the Path of Faith," which he presented at Franciscan University Steubenville on October 15, 2017 (this paper is not yet published).

Cavadini—on Augustine's behalf—is equal parts hopeful and direct. "Let me hasten to point out that there is a remedy," he writes,

> which is charity or love—the only thing that can shake the imagi-
> nation, even shock the imagination, out of its addiction to fame
> and prestige and free it to be able to rethink cultural conventions
> of excellence without fear of loss of status, position, job, or even,
> at the extreme, life. In charity we are free to give up prestige of our
> accomplishments because we come to love the Creator more than
> the creature [we might also say "truth" rather than "oneself"], or
> rather love the creature *in* the love of the Creator; and so we are
> free to speak up and speak out, free to critique the assumptions
> of excellence on which the very prestige attaching to our own ac-
> complishments is based.[24]

It turns out that it is not enough to form the mind according to appeals to "excellence." In truth, the responsibility of the university is to her-
ald what is truly worthy of pursuit, what ultimately measures excellence,
and what provides final liberation. By an Augustinian reading, there are
only two options for responding to this question: prestige or charity. To
lust after prestige is always to make oneself prey to the dominant power
structure, whereas the pursuit of charity as truth has the potential to free
one from the desire to be praised.

Cavadini knows, however, that Augustine as a "saint of suspicion" is
not quite done diagnosing the dangers of the culture of prestige. In fact, an
Augustinian reading also allows one to see that even acts of charity may be
coopted by the hankering for praise. As Cavadini continues, "The works of
love on their own are just as vulnerable to distortion as any other accomplishment: we await the congratulation of others, we love being thanked
and being praised instead of thanking and praising, or at least we expect an
even exchange—after all, what's fair is fair—and so pride subverts the one
and only way out, once again."[25]

This is where all those seemingly noble goals of modern universities receive their final critique. Even when the mission is to promote the
wellbeing of society, or to make groundbreaking discoveries in the name
of progress, or to educate students to make an impact on the world, the
trap of excellence is still ready to spring. Aiming at "justice" or "equality"
does not dismantle that trap. Even unspecified goals for contributing to

24. Cavadini, "Augustine."
25. Cavadini, "Augustine."

the "common good" are under surveillance. Why? Because there is always, always, always the temptation to want to be recognized as the student, the alumnus, the scholar, or the institution that made the contribution. "This institution is excellent because it is the one that does x, y, or z." Nothing is free of the trap of excellence except the willingness to give up the very claim to excellence itself—that is, to offer thanks.

Here is what Cavadini understands to be the special contribution of the Catholic university, which is by its identity and mission meant to be distinct from secular institutions. For secular universities, the "pursuit of truth for its own sake" would be a form of maintaining a posture of openness towards seeking a final end. That is, such institutions cannot and should not make a definitive claim as to what that end in fact is. A Catholic university, however, contains all that the secular university does but makes a special contribution: it proposes an ultimate (and foundational) claim by pointing toward and contemplating divine charity as the mystery upholding and guiding all that is. In Cavadini's words,

> The charity or love that can free us from addiction to our own destruction in the pursuit of [prestige]. . . is not, in the first instance, our own. Rather, it is something we hear about—for faith "comes through hearing" (Rom 10:17)—when we hear of the story of the Creator's loving descent into finitude and history: into finitude as a helpless baby, as vulnerable, naked, and non-prestigious as any other; and into history as the mess of corruption and fraud and betrayal that we have made of history—a descent without reserve and with no special exemptions for himself, as vulnerable to mocking laughter and spitting and slapping and betrayal and torture and murder as anyone who speaks up and speaks out against the prestigious of this world who have substituted their own canons of excellence for truth.[26]

As a *university*, a Catholic university brings the mind to form through the integration of its disciplines, and as a *Catholic* institution, it seeks both scholarship of and a witness to what the source and summit of truth is. Rather than curtailing the freedom of thought, this contemplation of divine, incarnate charity is the key that unlocks the trap of excellence sprung from the pedagogy of prestige. It is not the business of Catholic universities to form saints, but it is their business to present sanctity as the Catholic vision of human flourishing.

---

26. Cavadini, "Augustine." See also Cavadini, "Brief Reflection."

What does Catholic higher education look like when ordered to divine charity? Working that out is the challenge of building a great Catholic university in the modern age. The key point, though, is that this mission is the only one worth pursuing for Catholic higher education: where the pursuit of excellence is united to the remembrance of the unmerited gift that finds a home in students and scholars in wholeness of mind and thickness of character as "virtue."

4

The *Caritas* of Justice
The Eucharistic Charter of the Catholic University

TIMOTHY P. O'MALLEY

A PRESUMPTION EXISTS AMONG those involved in Catholic education that Catholic social doctrine provides a neutral ground whereby secular academics and religiously committed Catholic scholars can engage one another while avoiding particular doctrinal truth claims that have little place in the public sphere. The pursuit of a just society, for example, functions as a common denominator between a Catholic political scientist and a religiously agnostic political scientist. Community-based learning becomes a neutral space where religious and non-religious students alike engage in the task of transforming self and society.[1]

The purpose of this essay is not to offer an absolute denial of the merits of these assumptions. After all, the pursuit of justice in the Catholic university can become a space where humane learning, even among secular colleagues, encounters "the serious teaching of Christianity."[2] The Catholic university has a responsibility to bring the tools of various sciences to investigate the problems of poverty, of social inequality, of political insta-

---

1. Thompson, *Reason and Tolerance*, 147–72.
2. Buckley, *Catholic University as Promise and Project*, 127.

bility, and of human rights. To claim otherwise is to relegate the Catholic university to a sectarian enterprise in which religiously devout students have their identity affirmed at the same time that the University surrenders its public vocation.

From the perspective of the *Catholic university*, the problem is not so much that secular and religious colleagues should work together around the promotion of justice. Rather, it is the assumption that pure reason can function as an appropriate stand-in for the truth claims of divine Revelation, thus accommodating Catholic social doctrine to an imagined "neutral" space.[3] Such an assumption is an act of secularization whereby the divine Revelation is limited to the horizon of justice, resulting in a harmonization that brackets out the salvific virtuosity of Catholicism.[4] Certainly, Catholic social doctrine assumes the purification of reason made possible through divine Revelation.[5] It assumes that one can grasp the ultimate end of human existence insofar as one has gazed upon the self-giving love of the Word made flesh. Without the accompanying divine Revelation, Catholic social doctrine falls prey to the perils of a fallen reason in which justice is reduced to a will to power, an occasion in which the strongest win.

This essay challenges the assumption that Catholic social doctrine is the neutral common ground that makes the Catholic university acceptable to its secular interlocutors. The argument proceeds in three steps. First, it examines the methodological assumptions of Catholic social doctrine as articulated by the *Compendium of the Social Doctrine of the Church*. From the beginning, one discovers that Catholic social doctrine is integral to divine Revelation rather than a culturally acceptable translation of Christian truth claims. Second, the argument proceeds to claim that the *revealed* quality of Catholic social doctrine is good news for human inquiry within the university insofar as it allows for a renewed epistemic humility. Human action in the world, including the pursuit of justice, always involves power. And the Church provides a series of social teachings that grounds this pursuit of justice in the primordial act of love of the sacrifice of the Word made flesh. Lastly, the essay concludes by arguing for the Eucharistic charter of the Catholic university. Here, one is arguing not merely for the presence

3. Milbank, *Word Made Strange*, 268–92.

4. Here, one can perceive a Catholic equivalent to the erasure of religious identity among Protestant colleges and universities in the United States. See Marsden, *Soul of the American University*, 156–59.

5. Benedict XVI, *Deus Caritas Est*, par. 28a.

of Eucharistic liturgies on campus as acts of private devotion. Instead, it is only through the wedding feast of the Lamb that any act of justice can pass over from the will to power to a true sacrifice of love.

THE REVELATION OF CATHOLIC SOCIAL DOCTRINE

Catholic social doctrine is not a Kantian reduction of Catholicism to a series of reasonable ethical claims accessible to any rational person of good will.[6] Rather, the social doctrine of the Church arises from the particular encounter with divine Revelation made accessible through Jesus Christ. The salvation made available through the Paschal Mystery of Jesus Christ is to permeate "this world in the realities of the economy and labor, of technology and communications, of society and politics, of the international community and the relations among cultures and peoples."[7] That is, the world is to become a space of an economy of gift and love, rather than efficiency and power.

Left to reason alone, no human being could arrive at the doctrine of the preferential option for the poor. This is not because it is impossible for human reason to determine a rationale relative to the social benefits of ending poverty. Social scientists have rightly argued that early intervention in cases of childhood poverty within the United States can assist both impoverished children and society as a whole.[8] Through reasoned scientific inquiry, it is possible to argue for the wisdom of devoting more national resources to the reduction of poverty.

The social good of devoting more attention to those trapped in poverty is not yet a sufficient expression of the preferential option for the poor. As John Cavadini has written, "Contrary to popular belief, the 'preferential option for the poor' is first and foremost a doctrine about God, and not about the poor."[9] Catholics exercise a preferential option for the poor because God has first chosen the poor, those on the margins to be the beneficiaries of divine love: "Christ the Savior showed compassion in this regard, identifying himself with the 'least' among men (cf. Matt 25:40, 45)."[10] The doctrine of the preferential option for the poor is never discernable by pure

---

6. Kant, *Religion within the Boundaries of Pure Reason*, 174–75.

7. Pontifical Council, *Compendium of the Social Doctrine of the Church*, par. 1.

8. See Lynch, *Exceptional Returns*.

9. Cavadini, "Social Justice and Love," 3.

10. Pontifical Council, *Compendium of the Social Doctrine of the Church*, par. 182.

reason precisely because no human being could imagine the mercy made manifest in the totality of divine love upon the cross.

Catholic social doctrine, thus, relies upon the act of divine Revelation to make its particular claims relative to what constitutes salvation in the world. In the first chapter of the *Compendium of Catholic Social Doctrine*, this methodological assumption is made manifest. Human beings are necessarily religious creatures, capable of recognizing the gratuitousness of the created order and the subsequent responsibilities that come with abiding within the space of such a gift.[11] In Israel, this form of gratuity is lived out through obedience to the gift of the Law: "The gift of freedom and the Promised Land, and the gift of the Covenant on Sinai and the Ten Commandments are therefore intimately linked to the practices which must regulate, in justice and solidarity, the development of Israelite society."[12] The divine mercy of the Law, the gratuitous manifestation of God's will among human beings, necessitates the return gift of love that is worshipful obedience to the Law. divine Revelation heals human activity, restoring men and women to a posture of gratitude.

Jesus Christ, as fully divine and human, incarnates in his very being the gratuity of divine love and the appropriate human response. In the Incarnation of the Word made flesh:

> God's gratuitous love for humanity is revealed, before anything else, as love springing from the Father, from whom everything draws its source; as the free communication that the Son makes of this love, giving himself anew to the Father and giving himself to mankind; as the ever new fruitfulness of divine love that the Holy Spirit pours forth into the hearts of men (cf. Rom 5:5).[13]

Divine love has become manifest in the powerlessness of the Word made flesh. Human existence, as evident in the commandment of Christ to love one another, is now oriented toward communion in love rather than the exercise of the will to power. The *Compendium* concludes from this brief account of salvation history, "*The commandment of mutual love, which represents the law of life for God's people, must inspire, purify, and elevate all human relationships in society and in politics.*"[14] The meaning of creation is love unto the end, and the disciple of Christ is the one who through per-

---

11. Pontifical Council, *Compendium of the Social Doctrine of the Church*, par. 20.

12. Pontifical Council, *Compendium of the Social Doctrine of the Church*, par. 23.

13. Pontifical Council, *Compendium of the Social Doctrine of the Church*, par. 31.

14. Pontifical Council, *Compendium of the Social Doctrine of the Church*, par. 33.

sonal conversion brings "the appropriate remedies to institutions and living conditions when they are an inducement to sin, so that they conform to the norms of justice and advance the good rather than hinder it."[15] Catholic social doctrine responds to the human tendency to abuse power, to seize control, by attuning the human family to the logic of sacrificial love made manifest through Christ Jesus.

Catholic social doctrine is thus not a translation of divine Revelation into terms accommodated to the secular person. Instead, it is the political, ethical, and social consequences of the revelation to humanity of the totality of divine love made available through Jesus Christ. The freedom, for example, of someone to oppose unjust political laws emerges not simply from a philosophical account of free will but through a proper understanding of human authority vis-à-vis Jesus Christ's loving kingship over creation.[16] Through the divine Revelation of what constitutes authentic authority, the Church can and will engage in public argument relative to the freedom of the human person to offer worship to God alone: "The dignity of the person and the very nature of the quest for God requires that all men and women should be free from every constraint in the area of religion."[17] Persons of good will can enter into dialogue with the Church on the possibility of this religious freedom. But Catholic social doctrine comes about through a deeper reflection on the nature of divine Revelation itself and its subsequent consequences for human existence in the world.

Pope Francis's *Laudato si'* is an icon of this method of reflection. Human beings, gazing at creation, have the capacity to perceive creation as a gift that must be received rather than as a series of objects to be manipulated through human power. Thus, Pope Francis begins with a description of what is happening within creation, reading the "signs of the times." But he follows this social analysis not with further philosophical arguments about technology but a turn toward the Gospel of creation:

> The best way to restore men and women to their rightful place, putting an end to the absolute dominion over the earth, is to speak once more of the figure of a Father who creates and who alone owns the world. Otherwise, human beings will always try to impose their own laws and interests on reality.[18]

15. Pontifical Council, *Compendium of the Social Doctrine of the Church*, par. 42.

16. Pontifical Council, *Compendium of the Social Doctrine of the Church*, par. 383, 399–400.

17. Pontifical Council, *Compendium of the Social Doctrine of the Church*, 422.

18. Francis, "Laudato si'," par. 75.

It is the Church's doctrine of creation that is the key source for responding to the ecological crisis of the present age—one caused by a noxious mistake about humanity's role in cosmos.

Thus, the Church's Catholic social doctrine is not a neutral space apart from divine Revelation. Rather, such doctrine is a sustained reflection on the political, social, economic, and ethical consequences of a world ordered toward communion in Christ. It is only through contemplating the divine love made manifest in creation, salvation, and the ultimate end of humanity in eternal life, that the Church has something to offer at all relative to the social sphere. For the Church offers a vision of the common good, of the demands of solidarity as lived within community, because she has first encountered the love of God made manifest in Christ.

Such a claim raises an important question. Namely, if Catholic social doctrine is dependent on the act of divine Revelation, is it appropriate within the contemporary university at all? Can a university, dedicating itself to research and teaching, discern in the mystery of salvation made available to Christ the heart of its mission to the world? Such a question touches the core of the endangered status of the Catholic university among its peers in the contemporary academy. Catholic Social Teaching is considered allowable within many Catholic colleges and universities because it is considered a socially acceptable form of religious expression compared to other doctrinal, doxological, or moral truth claims. Put crassly, *New York Times* columnists are pleased to praise the Church's commitment to social justice, while bracketing the Trinitarian or Christological foundations to such ethical action.

Catholic social doctrine, ironically, becomes not a neutral space where the believer may encounter the unbeliever in the pursuit of truth. Instead, it becomes a space that necessitates that the believer (whether professor or student) bracket out religious commitment, relegating it to private deeds of prayer or liturgical worship. Without a horizon grounded in the self-giving love of the Word made flesh, the university now aspires to "do good" (whatever that means) rather than to offer appropriate worship in light of God's generosity. The creation of a supposed neutral space of Catholic social doctrine, one that brackets divine Revelation, will culminate in the foundation of erstwhile Catholic institutions that offer encomia to ethical behavior rather than reasonable praise to Jesus Christ.

THE REASONABLENESS OF LOVE

But may a Catholic university *reasonably* describe itself as grounded in an act of divine Revelation rather than principles that are agreeable to those who do not believe? Is the *reasonable* pursuit of justice, however defined, not a safer space for engaging in dialogue with society as a whole?

The first question necessitates a defense of the reasonableness of Revelation to begin with. The goal cannot be to offer a philosophical apologetics for the fittingness of the Creed, the manner in which the kerygma should infuse every discipline. This way of answering the question would again risk a sectarianism in which engagement with the world is made an impossible task. Rather, it is necessary to show how openness to divine Revelation *in se* is in the more reasonable position to begin with. To commence from the event of divine Revelation is a liberation of reason rather than its imprisonment, allowing for the proper use of reason in questions related to justice. Catholic social doctrine, beginning from Revelation, is in fact a purification of the act of reason.

The French philosopher, Jean-Luc Marion, has taken up the purification of reason through the contemplation of divine Revelation. In his essay, "Faith and Reason," Marion describes two problems with naked reason in the modern age. He writes:

> To each science there . . . corresponds a method of constitution and of production of objects . . . [and] modern rationality unfolds by ceaselessly enlarging the number and range of such objects. Not only does it constitute them intellectually and realize them experimentally, but it produces and reproduces them technically, in such a way that a new world of technical objects has sprung up before our increasingly less surprised eyes. . . . This change has defined the common rationality of our reason and is extended to nature, whose "masters and possessors" we become.[19]

Modern rationality,[20] for example, gazes at the problem of poverty and begins to assign causes. The assessment of such causes may be endless, resulting in further objective studies through the disciplines of political economy and sociology. The rational person, gazing at poverty from a distance, begins to offer technical solutions to the problem ranging from

19. Marion, *Believing in Order to See*, 7.

20. For Marion, modern rationality is defined as a radical separation between the object of knowing and the subjective knower. Here, Marion is critical of what he sees as Descartes's mistake. See Marion, *On Descartes's Passive Thought*.

the redistribution of income to tax credits for middle and lower class families. In these cases, there is an objective abstractness to poverty necessary for scientific inquiry. The "poor" become a group of human beings to be analyzed, studied, and understood for the sake of technical improvement. In this context, it is easily forgotten that these "poor" are concrete human beings rather than ciphers whereby public intellectuals make arguments relative to the best way to govern the *polis*. The danger of academic inquiry is that it forgets that political and social analysis pertains to the functioning of the use of power by fallen creatures upon concrete human bodies: families and local communities of tradition.[21]

Such inquiry by reason alone also suffers from inattention to the concreteness of human experience and personhood. As Marion notes, this assumed objectivity is not inclusive of what it means to be a human being in the world. Human beings do not simply gaze at creation objectively but are immersed in the created order as enfleshed beings. Such enfleshment, for Marion means that:

> we do not stand opposite ourselves, but sense what we are and are what we sense in the closest, namely pain and pleasure, death and birth, hunger and thirst, sleep and fatigue, but also hatred and love, communion and division, justice and violence. From this, from what is closest, we know very clearly that the common rationality of objects knows nothing and is of no help.[22]

In the end, the objective researcher cannot stand outside of his or her human condition to suggest technical improvements for society. The act of reason is always being performed by persons who abide in a space between justice and violence, between known and unknown desires. The "reasonable" person must recognize that he or she is always born into a received world, one that has shaped every dimension of his or her experience. One can no more stand outside of this enfleshed and thus historical nature in thinking about justice than a fish can attempt to survey the existence of light apart from water.

Left to the sphere of naked reason, bracketing out the enfleshed nature of existence, all that remains is the individual or political will to power. Marion writes:

21. Ward, *Politics of Discipleship*, 27.
22. Marion, *Believing in Order to See*, 8.

What is the point of the humanity of humans, the naturalness of nature, the justice of the city and the truth of knowledge? Why not rather their opposites, the dehumanization of humans for improving humanity, the systematic bleeding of nature in order to develop the economy, injustice so as to render society more efficient, the absolute empire of information-distraction in order to escape the constraints of the true?[23]

Marion's questions are not quite as apocalyptic as they seem. If seeking justice begins through reason alone, through the performance of technique, then could one not argue for the reasonableness of violence for the sake of greater justice among the human family?[24] Could one not "reason" their way to the employment of propaganda to convince the nation-state to act in a way that the well educated presume necessary for the flourishing of justice?[25] Is there not an epistemological hubris in presuming that any human being can pursue the ends of justice and know, beyond a shadow of a doubt, that justice has been accomplished—especially when such justice is performed by a state more interested in pursuing power rather than virtue?[26]

Reason alone does not rely upon the gift of the person or a particular tradition in making an assessment. Naked reason stands outside of the community, outside of embodiment, to determine the best course of action. Justice, in order to be virtuous, must have some notion of the good, some first principles through which the actors of power operate lest just become nothing but the will to power.[27]

An example of the employment of "reasonable" justice is the use of leisure within the *polis* to put an end to violence. Global cities can be violent places where human beings of different ethnic groups and financial backgrounds live within the same space. In these cities, downtowns are often redeveloped for the leisure class, eliminating poor men and women in a process of gentrification that makes the neighborhood "safe." But such safety is given not through an authentic encounter with values, with any sense of the good life, but instead through the sports complex, the mall, or

---

23. Marion, *Believing in Order to See*, 9.

24. Such a question is at the heart of Jacque Ellul's critique against "Christians for violence" in Ellul, *Violence*, 27–80.

25. See Ellul, *Propaganda*.

26. Ellul, *Political Illusion*, 185–98.

27. Milbank and Pabst, *Politics of Virtue*, 5.

the shopping area that pacifies human violence.[28] In the act of increasing flow of financial capital into a particular city, the poor (often communities of color) are simply "reasonably" eliminated from the area so that property values can increase, so that like-minded human beings can go to Chipotle and Urban Outfitters in peace. This is not justice, even if it generates more tax revenue to the city for the sake of schools. Left to reason alone, why would a city forego the opportunity for seeking profit above maintaining local communities that are often erased in the process of gentrification.[29]

The problem with naked reason is that it reduces the human person to the illusion of creator rather than recipient of identity. The only object of concern of the human being is the creation of a future world constructed by the enlightened person rather than receiving existence itself as gift. As Joseph Ratzinger writes, "By thinking only of the practicable, of what can be made, [humanity] is in danger of forgetting to reflect on [itself] and on the meaning of . . . existence."[30] Such calculating thought refuses a reflective task, one in which the question of meaning rather than efficiency is central. It refuses to think about the consequences of human activity, about the values that undergirds action.

For Marion, Christians have a particular gift to offer to the *aporia* posed by modern reasoning: Jesus Christ. Christians do not uphold the primacy of abstract, reasonable justice in human relationships. Christians cannot succumb to the totalitarianism of calculating thought. Instead, Marion concludes that Christians can offer only the totalizing love of God made manifest through Jesus Christ, a supersaturated love that is reasonable. He writes, "For the love revealed by the Word, hence by the *Logos*, unfolds as a *logos*, thus as a reason. And it is a reason by full right because it allows us to reach the closest and the innermost phenomena, those experienced by flesh and those that intuition saturates."[31] Jesus Christ is the Word made flesh, the manifestation that salvation comes not through escaping the human body but entering more deeply into the facticity of enfleshment. The transformation of reason provided by Jesus Christ is not just a check

28. Ward, *Politics of Discipleship*, 218.

29. Gentrification, importantly, is not simply a matter of individual consumers deciding to live within a city. Gentrification, as Peter Moskowitz writes, "is a system that places the needs of capital (both in terms of city budget and in terms of real estate profits) above the needs of people" (Moskowitz, *How to Kill a City*, 9). See Moskowitz, *How to Kill a City*.

30. Ratzinger, *Introduction to Christianity*, 71.

31. Marion, *Believing in Order to See*, 10–11.

against reason's excess. Instead, God is love in the flesh, and therefore the act of reasoning as an embodied creature made in the image and likeness of this incarnate God must be suffused with this received love. There is a transformation of the act of thinking through engagement with theology, with the wisdom revealed through the Resurrection.[32]

In this sense, the Catholic university has a particular vocation in the promotion of justice. The goal is not simply to develop a more just society, to "do good," a task accomplishable by any research University in the United States in the twenty-first century. Left to its own devices, to its own reason, the "good" that the Catholic university can accomplish might actually be quite harmful. Instead, the Catholic university seeks to understand what is just for particular human beings through the self-giving love of the Word made flesh. It is only through the totalizing love of God that human beings can begin to perceive anew the possibility of justice in society as gift. Justice is the result of human beings willing to engage in the hard work of gazing with love upon fellow persons, not reducing them to objects in some argumentative language game in the field of economics, political science, or sociology.[33] Justice is not merely a matter of financial, class, or racial equity. It is, within Christianity, love.

In this sense, the revelation that God is love is the source of reason's reform. Ideas about justice can be wrong. They can have devastating consequences for humanity that no human being can perceive. They can function as idols of power whereby the "in-group" establishes what is "just" precisely because it is also politically and financially expedient. As Benedict XVI comments, the practical reasoning of politics "must undergo constant purification, since it can never be completely free of the danger of a certain ethical blindness caused by the dazzling effect of power and special interests."[34] It is only the totality of divine love that can heal reason of this desire for control, for the exertion of a will to power.

The gift of divine love at the heart of the Catholic university does not mean that the University has as its sole obligation the preaching of Jesus Christ, ignoring the intellectual life or modern thought for pious musings. Rather, the task is to determine how every dimension of human existence

32. Falque, *Crossing the Rubicon*, 132–33.

33. For this reason, justice within Catholicism involves not merely a concept or intellectual schema but rather an encounter with a concrete person, lest it become a form of idolatry. See Marion, *Prolegomena to Charity*, 71–101.

34. Benedict XVI, *Deus Caritas Est*, par. 28a.

has a surplus of meaning, of possibility because of what has been revealed through the love of God. The human is transfigured through encounter within the divine. And it is within the Eucharistic liturgy, in particular, that the Catholic university discovers its mission for a *Logos*-centered justice.

THE EUCHARISTIC CHARTER OF THE CATHOLIC UNIVERSITY

The presence of the Eucharist at the heart of the Catholic university can be easily problematized. The Eucharist is, of course, the *most* Catholic of Catholic actions, the one that would likely exclude the person of good will from participating. Students, who may be attracted to the corporal works of mercy and to the transformation of the world through justice might be nonplussed to discover that the Mass that they never attend is the source of their commitment to the poor. The "prudent" Catholic university would place a radical separation between the works of justice and the Mass, so as to allow students and faculty interested in Catholic social doctrine to pursue this work while leaving Eucharistic devotion to the pious. When appropriate, such devotional Catholics should be urged to care about the plight of the immigrant or the end of poverty. But the view is that liturgical attendance is a private decision that the university may publicly praise but could not place as central to its humanizing endeavor as the pursuit of justice.

The root problem of this objection is that it does not emerge from a sufficient encounter with the public nature of Eucharistic action.[35] At many Catholic universities, the Mass is treated as the private act of the few, devoted citizens of the Church who escape from the *polis* to encourage the transcendent God outside of space. But such analysis passes over the cosmic and thus political dimensions of Eucharistic performance. The Eucharist is not a private devotional activity pertaining to mere transcendence but the entrance of the Church as the leaven of humanity into the sacrificial love of God. The Eucharistic rites of the Church are part of the purification of reason through love.

The Mass is the source of justice for the Catholic university, first and foremost, because it is through the Eucharistic liturgy that the Church and thus the world receive and become the sacrificial gift of divine love.

---

35. For an exception to this tendency, see Cavanaugh, *Theopolitical Imagination*.

Christian worship is never private. As Joseph Ratzinger writes in his *The Spirit of the Liturgy*:

> Christian liturgy is never just an event organized by a particular group or set of people or even by a particular local Church. Mankind's movement toward Christ meets Christ's movement toward men. He wants to unite mankind and bring about the one Church, the one divine assembly, of all men. Everything, then, comes together: the horizontal and the vertical, the uniqueness of God and the unity of mankind, the communion of all who worship in spirit and in truth.[36]

In the Eucharist, the totality of Christ's love is given through the transformation of bread and wine into Body and Blood. This act of self-giving love, made present in the Eucharistic mystery, is not reducible to a supersaturated phenomenon that renders humanity mute before the mystery. The totality of love is what actually enables the operation of human freedom. The sacrifice of the Mass, what Ratzinger describes as divinization, is "the healing of wounded freedom, atonement, purification, deliverance from estrangement . . . it assumes the aspect of healing, the loving transformation of broken freedom, of painful expiation."[37] To participate in the Mass is not a private activity of a single, devoted Christian. It is instead the process of offering the entirety of human freedom unto God through the act of communion.

Such communion is between God and person, between person and all humanity. For the sacrificial love at the heart of the Eucharist is linked closely to the offering of the entire body, the entire self unto God through communion with the Church. In *Deus Caritas Est*, Benedict XVI clarifies this "sacramental mysticism" as intrinsically social in orientation. He writes:

> Communion draws me out of myself toward him, and thus also toward unity with all Christians. . . . Love of God and love of neighbor are now truly united: God incarnate draws us all to himself. . . . Faith, worship, and *ethos* are interwoven as a single reality which takes shape in our encounter with God's *agape*. . . . "Worship" itself, Eucharistic communion, includes the reality both of being loved and of loving others in turn. A Eucharist which does not pass over into the concrete practice of love is intrinsically fragmented.[38]

36. Ratzinger, *Spirit of the Liturgy*, 30.
37. Ratzinger, *Spirit of the Liturgy*, 19.
38. Benedict XVI, *Deus Caritas Est*, par. 14.

Here, Benedict is not simply saying that there are social consequences to receiving the Eucharist. Instead, the very logic of Eucharistic communion, of entrance into freeing and loving worship of God, is the transformation of the world into a space of love. The human being, born within a family, abiding within a political community, educated in a society, is to transform each of these arenas into a space where love can reign. Such transformation is not reducible, for Benedict, to personal acts of love alone but include configuring social life so that it resembles the worshipful wisdom of the crucified God.[39] It is a form of social justice infused from the beginning with divine *caritas*.

The Eucharist, thus, forms the Catholic university into that divine *caritas* that infuses all human activity. Such Eucharistic transformation is intrinsic to the intellectual evangelization that the university carries out insofar as the university becomes a space ordered first and foremost to divine and thus human communion before it becomes a space of technical mastery. At the heart of the university is a mystery of poverty that human reason cannot master. In describing the Eucharist, the Jewish philosopher Simone Weil claims:

> The virtue of the dogma of the real presence lies in its very absurdity. Except for the infinitely touching symbolism of food, there is nothing in a morsel of bread that can be associated with our thought of God. Thus the conventional character of the divine presence is evident. Christ can be present in such an object only by convention. For this very reason he can be perfectly present in it. God can only be present in secret here below. His presence in the Eucharist is truly secret since no part of our thought can reach the secret. Thus it is total.[40]

Mere bread becomes the living presence of God, inaccessible to the human senses. The university, no matter the technical expertise of its faculty and staff, cannot master this mystery of divine donation. The "conventional" nature of the Eucharist necessitates that the gift of presence precedes human reception of this love. Human beings, through Eucharistic devotion, are formed to await the arrival of the gift rather than seize love. Such contemplative openness to love is present in the student seeking wisdom in an ancient text, just as much as the one who seeks to enact policies that uphold the dignity of the immigrant.

39. Benedict XVI, *Deus Caritas Est*, par. 29.
40. Weil, *Awaiting God*, 121–22.

The Eucharist operates according to a logic that the University must keep in its heart as it performs acts of justice. The goal is not technical mastery first! Instead, it is the attentive gaze of love, attending to the dignity of the human person that may not be visible to the senses, which may not be immediately accessible to reason. A Catholic university, formed according to a Eucharistic pedagogy, will not let itself be taken over by the logic of the market or power politics. Through the pursuit of truth, always through love, the Catholic university perceives possibilities for loving attention in unexpected places—among the persecuted, among those suffering the effects of racism and classism, and in the mundane existence of nuptial life.

This Eucharistic pedagogy, for the Catholic university, is not didactic even if it is centered around the *Logos*, the enfleshment of the Word in the human body. Instead, the Eucharistic pedagogy of the Church is embodied, personal, bringing every dimension of human existence into relationship with God. As the Catholic philosopher and theologian Emmanuel Falque argues:

> Christians . . . cannot simply be content with loving one another. . . . They must also, and particularly when it is a question of the eucharist, look forward with one another . . . to be incorporated in the resurrected Word. It is neither an individual nor a community that is called to be humanized in the resurrected Son, but the whole of humanity—to go, in other words, from that Chaos that is rightly brought to light in the eros, to the cosmos that is also lived by the apape.[41]

Justice, eucharisticized in the Catholic university, is part of a broader project whereby the entire human condition is made divine through the Eucharist. The pragmatism of justice within the limits of reason alone fails to recognize the wounded nature of the human condition *in toto*. The Catholic university enacts a divine and thus "just" transformation of the cosmos through cultivating a Christian humanism in which every dimension of human experience is contemplated in light of divine *agape*.

In other words, in the Eucharistic pedagogy of the Church, the senses matter. A Catholic university educates in Catholic social doctrine not merely through an abstract study of principles, of case studies drawn from political science or sociology. Instead, a Eucharistic approach to justice forms men and women capable of bringing the entirety of their humanity as lived out in family, society, and in the political realm to the Word made

41. Falque, *Wedding Feast of the Lamb*, 58.

flesh. Working for justice in these situations is closely linked to concrete care for human flesh. For the concrete flesh of the unborn child and the immigrant, suffering the effects of calculating rather than reflective thought.

CONCLUSION

Therefore, Catholic social doctrine is not reducible to a neutral space where Catholics and non-Catholics can agree on a series of lowest common denominators. Instead, Catholic social doctrine is a matter of divine Revelation, the process whereby men and women think through the consequences of divine *caritas* for every dimension of human life. It is a purification of reason alone, one that grounds human thought not in abstract concepts that may become idols but in the concrete iconicity of loving concrete, existing, bodily persons in the world.

The Eucharist is not an optional dimension for those seeking to educate students in the rudiments of this social doctrine. Instead, it is that necessary encounter with the totality of divine love, the communion with the triune God that enables human beings to become this love for the cosmos.

The Eucharistic pedagogy of the Church does not exist alongside the exercise of social justice within the university. Instead, the Eucharist functions as the charter of the Catholic university that enables it to contemplate existence not through the lens of power politics and technique but through the reasonable foolishness of love.

If the Catholic university does not uphold its Eucharistic charter, it will discover that its pursuit of justice, of "doing good," quickly becomes simply another exercise of the will to power rather than a response of contemplative, patient, merciful love.

PART 2

In the Name of Truth:
The Idea of a University

5

What Makes a University Catholic?

John Garvey

THE BLUEPRINT FOR BUILDING a great university is fairly simple.[1] It is like the plan for building a great baseball team: hire great players. In a fundamental sense, the faculty are the university. Students pay to learn what they profess. If the faculty are great scholars and teachers, the university will be great.

The blueprint for building a Catholic university is also simple. It was laid out in 1990 by John Paul II in the apostolic constitution *Ex corde ecclesiae*. John Paul was himself a university professor, so he knew how universities worked. *Ex corde* runs almost fifty pages in the English translation; but the kernel of the document is four short lines near the end. In Part II, a section titled "General Norms," John Paul says that in order for a university to be Catholic, a majority of its faculty must be Catholic.

What I most admire about this prescription is its modesty. John Paul did not say that he and the other bishops should superintend the Catholic character of Catholic universities. On the contrary, he began his observations about the university community by conceding that "the responsibility for maintaining and strengthening the Catholic identity of the university rests primarily with the university itself."[2] Bishops are not academics.

---

1. This essay first appeared in *Commonweal* magazine in February 2017. It is reprinted here with the permission of *Commonweal* and the author.

2. John Paul II, "Ex Corde Ecclesiae," III.4.1.

(John Paul and Benedict XVI were exceptions.) *Ex corde* says to university faculties and administrators, in effect, "We don't know how to run a Catholic university. That's your job. The only thing we insist on is that you choose Catholics to do it."

This is, as I say, a fairly simple plan. If a university follows it, it will be Catholic. If it does not, it will not. But it has met with resistance in the academy. I want to discuss one line of argument against it that I find both powerful and well considered, but wrong.

A MULTITUDE OF TONGUES

Harry Keyishian was an adjunct English professor at the University of Buffalo in the 1960s. The university was once a private school, founded by Millard Fillmore (this was before he became president) in 1846. But in 1962 it merged into the New York state university system. That made Keyishian a state employee, subject to something called the Feinberg Law, which required him to sign a certificate saying he was not a Communist. I'm not sure whether he was or not, but Keyishian was at least scrupulous about signing the certificate, and so his contract was not renewed.

He sued the New York Board of Regents and won. The Supreme Court held that the Feinberg Law and several earlier New York sedition laws that it enforced were inconsistent with the academic freedom guaranteed by the Constitution. Here is how Justice William Brennan put it:

> The First Amendment . . . does not tolerate laws that cast a pall of orthodoxy over the classroom. . . . The classroom is peculiarly the "marketplace of ideas." The nation's future depends upon leaders trained through wide exposure to that robust exchange of ideas which discovers truth "out of a multitude of tongues, (rather) than through any kind of authoritative selection."[3]

Let us be careful in parsing this. It is not a postmodern argument. The Court does not say that all ideas deserve equal protection because one is as good as another, that there is no such thing as truth. It argues for a free market of ideas on instrumental grounds. If we want to discover the truth, Brennan says, we should prefer "a multitude of tongues" to "orthodoxy" and "authoritative selection."

---

3. "Keyishian v Board of Regents."

The most famous version of this argument is made by the utilitarian philosopher John Stuart Mill. Mill had this in common with Keyishian: when it came time for him to apply to college, he refused to subscribe to the Thirty-Nine Articles of the Church of England, and so was ineligible to attend Oxford or Cambridge. He went to University College, London.

On Liberty, the best known of Mill's political writings, was published in 1859, a little more than a hundred years before the *Keyishian* decision. Chapter 2 of *On Liberty* is an extended defense of the liberty of thought and discussion. Justice Brennan assumed that free trade in ideas was the surest path to truth. Mill offers three reasons why this may be so.

First, the opinions we suppress may turn out to be true. "All silencing of discussion is an assumption of infallibility." Think about Galileo and Urban VIII. Turns out the earth really does revolve around the sun. Second, it may be the case that "conflicting doctrines, instead of one being true and the other false, share the truth between them." Chemists in the nineteenth century debated whether inanimate catalysts or living cells caused fermentation. It turns out they were both right: it is caused by enzymes (inanimate bodies) pressed out of living cells. Third, suppose that the received opinion is entirely true. Unless we are forced to consider objections to it, Mill says, our reception of it will in time become a mindless and reflexive attachment. "Truth, thus held, is but one superstition the more accidentally clinging to the words which enunciate a truth."

You can probably see where this leads, in the discussion about *Ex corde ecclesiae* and building a great Catholic university. Some people draw from Mill and his disciples the conclusion that a great Catholic university is a contradiction in terms. If we hire a majority of Catholics (instead of a multitude of tongues), we will have a harder time discovering truth than schools that reject "orthodoxy" and "authoritative selection." Without dissent and disagreement, without the intellectual give and take that characterizes a free market of ideas, we are bound to lose our way and have no one to call us back.

Or so the argument goes. The funny thing is, it is easy to find examples of great universities that contradict Mill's thesis. Consider the University of Chicago. The Chicago School of Economics developed around Milton Friedman and George Stigler in the 1950s. It embraced a neoclassical approach to economics based on rational expectations. The Chicago School spun off parallel movements like Law and Economics and public-choice theory. The university's website lists twenty-eight Nobel Prize winners who spent some part of their careers at Chicago as faculty, students, or researchers.

In building up this great school Chicago preferred people who shared its peculiar orientation rather than Keynesian economists. They wanted faculty who believed in markets and worried more about government regulation than they did about private monopolies. Chicago was the very embodiment of free-market thinking, yet it did not seek a multitude of tongues for its faculty. Paul Douglas, once a professor at Chicago and later a US. senator, wrote that he left the university because economist Frank "Knight was openly hostile [to me], and his disciples seemed to be everywhere."

Here is another example. The Bauhaus School was an art school that operated in Germany from 1919 to 1933, when it was closed under pressure from the Nazis. It featured faculty like Walter Gropius, Hannes Meyer, Marcel Breuer, and Mies van der Rohe. Painters Paul Klee and Wassily Kandinsky joined in the 1920s. Bauhaus gave birth to architectural modernism, a style that features simple forms, a stress on function and rationality, and an effort to infuse mass production with artistic spirit. Think of the Pan Am building (Mies) or the Whitney Museum (Breuer) in New York, or the Lake Shore apartments in Chicago (Mies).

In building this school the directors sought faculty who shared their passion for newness. They did not want classical architects and painters. They were not interested in a baroque revival. They would not have hired Bernini. They liked flat roofs, right angles, and minimal ornamentation. They used dull colors—a lot of white and black. Bauhaus was a revolution that influenced a century of architecture. But the school was not assembled from a multitude of tongues.

I could add other counterexamples: the Yale School of literary criticism, the Cambridge School of political thought, the Frankfurt School of critical theory. What they all have in common is a dedication to a common project, usually a departure from some academic orthodoxy, and a sense that the group is working on its own to build something new. They all laid the foundations of great intellectual movements. And yet they were built up on principles that seem inconsistent with Mill's idea of academic freedom. In building their faculties, they did not seek out a multitude of tongues. How can this be?

AUTHORITY, COMPETENCIES, AND JUDGMENT

Building a great university is a complicated thing. There is some truth in Mill's thesis. But there is more to the project than that. Let me illustrate the point with a brief account of another of my intellectual heroes.

Michael Polanyi was the fifth child born into a family of secular Jews in Hungary in 1891. His father built railroads. His mother's father was the chief rabbi of Vilnius. He got a medical degree, then a Ph.D. in chemistry. (His son won the Nobel Prize in 1986.) In 1919 he converted to Christianity. In the 1920s he taught at the Kaiser Wilhelm Institute in Berlin. When the Nazis came to power in the 1930s he moved to England, where he taught at the University of Manchester until his retirement.

Though he was a pretty famous scientist, he is better known for his writings about epistemology and social science. In 1962 he gave a lecture at Chicago's Roosevelt University titled "The Republic of Science," about building intellectual communities. During and after World War II there were efforts in England to direct the progress of science into channels that would better serve the public welfare. Polanyi compared these to Soviet schemes for having the Academy of Science guide research, the better to support that country's Five-Year Plans.

Consider the case of Trofim Lysenko, a Soviet biologist who worked at improving wheat-crop yields during the Depression. Lysenko rejected the developing science of genetics as a product of bourgeois capitalism. He believed that acquired traits could be inherited. If this were true, it would allow fairly rapid reengineering of plant and animal life, so the theory appealed to the Soviet leadership. Lysenko became a protégé of Joseph Stalin. Scientists who disagreed with him were sent to the gulag. The result was the essential destruction of a branch of science in the Soviet Union for several decades.

Though Polanyi appreciated the sentiments that inspired these British and Soviet efforts, he found their aim misguided. Science is a particular kind of joint task that requires the spontaneous coordination of independent initiatives, not central control. Imagine, he says, that we have a very large jigsaw puzzle, and we are trying to put the pieces together in the shortest possible time. We can speed things up by hiring more helpers.

Notice, though, how this is different from hiring a dozen people to shell peas. There each worker can tend to her own pile. The total number of peas shelled will not vary if the workers are isolated from each other. With the jigsaw puzzle the helpers must work in sight of each other, so that each time one fits a piece in, the others can see what further steps become possible. This is what we mean by saying that their work is coordinated.

Even as their work is coordinated, it is also independent. If we try to organize the helpers' behavior under a single authority, we lose the benefit of their individual initiatives and "reduce their joint effectiveness to that of the single person directing them from the centre."[4] This is what happened with Lysenko in the Soviet Union.

This is a powerful argument for academic freedom. But I want you to notice three interesting things about it. First, it is implicit in the jigsaw-puzzle analogy that there is a correct solution. The pieces do not just fit together any which way. There is one right arrangement. Polanyi was no postmodern; he did not subscribe to epistemological and moral relativism. He believed that truth is real. But how do we know when we have found it? Who is to say?

This is the second interesting thing. If truth is real, there are right and wrong opinions, an "orthodoxy of science," as Polanyi puts it.[5] And if there is an orthodoxy, there is an authority to judge about it. It cannot be any single person. (That again is the lesson of Lysenko.) Rather, it is to be found in the scientific community, which is responsible for maintaining professional standards.

Though each scientist is competent to judge only about his own small corner of studies, he will have some sense about standards in immediately adjacent areas. If we consider the larger community of scientists, we will find a network of overlapping competencies that together generate uniform standards of scientific merit. Consider again the helpers working on the jigsaw puzzle. It would not work if each person had a different understanding of the job (if, for example, one person believed that puzzle pieces ought to be stacked rather than fitted together). The community of scholars must share the same idea of what problem they are working on, and what counts as a good solution.

This is the third point. For the community of scholars to be authoritative, there must be standards for admission to it. In Polanyi's view "the authority of science is essentially traditional."[6] It is transmitted from one generation to another the way artistic, moral, and legal traditions are transmitted. Scientists learn their trade by apprenticing with people who have

4. Polanyi, "Republic of Science," 3.
5. Polanyi, "Republic of Science," 6.
6. Polanyi, "Republic of Science," 16.

already mastered the tradition. To be accepted into the trade, they must submit to "a vast range of value-judgments" exercised over all the domains of science.[7]

Universities play a uniquely important role in the creation of this republic of science. The "justification for the pursuit of scientific research in universities," Polanyi says, "lies in the fact that the universities provide an intimate communion for the formation of scientific opinion, free from corrupting intrusions and distractions."[8]

DISCIPLINED CREATIVITY

You can see where I am going with this. *Ex corde ecclesiae* takes a similar approach to building a Catholic university. The encyclical does not undertake to regulate, Soviet style, the teaching of theology, or physics, or literature. It does not prefer or condemn particular theories or schools of thought. It does not say that an undergraduate curriculum must include twelve hours each of philosophy and theology. It says instead that:

> The responsibility for maintaining and strengthening the Catholic identity of the university rests primarily with the university itself. . . . This responsibility . . . calls for the recruitment of . . . personnel, especially teachers and administrators, who are both willing and able to promote that identity.[9]

The central thing John Paul insists on is that the people who build the university community be apprenticed in the Catholic tradition, as Polanyi's scientists were formed in the scientific tradition, and committed to the common project of building the Catholic intellectual life.

Building a Catholic faculty is not tribalism, any more than building a republic of science is. It is a recognition that, in order to create a distinctively Catholic intellectual culture, we need to build an intellectual community governed by a Catholic worldview. A shared commitment to Catholic ideas about Creation and Providence, of human beings made in the image of God, will spur creativity and the development of a culture that expresses these ideas.

7. Polanyi, "Republic of Science," 17.

8. Polanyi, "Republic of Science," 15.

9. John Paul II, "Ex Corde Ecclesiae," III.4.1.

Let me close the circle by returning to Mill's arguments. There is a distinction between embracing the Catholic tradition as a constitutional principle and regulating particular activities in research and teaching. Polanyi wrestled with this issue, too. There is an internal tension in science between the need to adhere to orthodox professional standards and the demand for originality in research: "The professional standards of science must impose a framework of discipline and at the same time encourage rebellion against it."[10] Kepler's theory of elliptical orbits grew out of an effort to defend Copernicus's ideas about uniform motion. Newton relied on Copernicus and Kepler to find answers unthinkable to them. The defense of originality does not demand the rejection of orthodoxy. On the contrary, it is impossible without it.

This is why *Ex corde ecclesiae* can include a stout defense of academic freedom alongside its insistence on hiring a predominantly Catholic faculty. It says: "The church . . . recognizes the academic freedom of scholars in each discipline in accordance with its own principles and proper methods."[11] This is not mere lip service to an ideal the secular academy prizes. The Church really means it. The process it favors for keeping the faith is not compulsion and censorship, but building up the body of Christ.

10. Polanyi, "Republic of Science," 6.
11. John Paul II, "Ex Corde Ecclesiae," I.3.29.

6

On the Conceptual Frameworks and Integration of Academic Disciplines

PETER KILPATRICK

IT IS A DISTINCT honor to write this essay for a volume honoring Professor John Cavadini, a good friend and colleague who has done much in the service of the Department of Theology, the discipline of theology, and for the Catholic and evangelizing mission of the University of Notre Dame. I write on the topic of the integration of the disciplines, and the conceptual and methodological frameworks relevant to each of the disciplines, with a special view to the discipline of engineering. This is a topic near and dear to me, but I will also address the whole idea of a University, as integrating the disciplines necessarily brings the larger issue into play.

THE UNIVERSITY AND THE MULTIVERSITY

As no less eminent a philosopher than Alasdair MacIntyre points out in his book *God, Philosophy, and Universities*, "any organized and institutionalized scheme of learning presupposes some view of how the various academic disciplines do or do not relate to each other."[1] All Universities presuppose a number of important things about how disciplines relate to

1. MacIntyre, *God, Philosophy, Universities*, 15.

each other and about the very nature of truth. This is no small issue and relates, I believe at least in part, to the larger issue of the current state of our public and civic discourse. If a large percentage of US citizens attend college or university and are taught, explicitly or implicitly, that the various disciplines within a university are largely unrelated, then perhaps those persons begin to think that, because I am a lawyer, or doctor, or bricklayer, or social worker, that the interests and the discipline of engineering are of no concern to me and my job. If this notion pervades the sentiments of a sufficiently high percentage of citizens, it is not difficult to imagine that this contributes in some measure to our current state of dysfunction in our civil discourse. My goal here is to offer some reflections specifically on how engineering and science relate to theology and philosophy (or should relate to each other) and how this might impact one's view of higher education and of the nature of truth.

Engineering as a Discipline

Engineering as a practice is as old as humankind. As I have defined it elsewhere,[2] engineering is the application of knowledge (in the modern age: science, math, and other skills and learnings) to design, build, and implement engineering artifacts for the *good of humankind.* Thus, engineering has a *telos,* a purpose, and hence a fundamental element of the study and practice of engineering is that it exists in order to design, create, and operate new products and processes to advance the human condition. For example, shelters, houses, buildings, and the entire "built environment" are all products of some kind of engineering, no matter how primitive or crude. Thus, humans have been practicing engineering in this sense for at least 10,000–15,000. Engineering as an academic discipline is still quite young, perhaps no more than 200–250 years old, although the "mechanical arts" were taught in the medieval schools as long ago as 700–800 years.

As academic engineering grew and developed, it became clear that the science and mathematics that underlay a particular aspect of engineering could be quite varied. For example, the branch of physics called mechanics (as developed by Isaac Newton and as harnessed by many who utilized the new invention of the steam engine to convert thermal energy into work) undergirds mechanical and structural engineering. Electromagnetism as developed by Maxwell is at the root of electrical engineering, and chemistry

2. Kilpatrick, "College of Engineering at Notre Dame."

obviously underlies chemical engineering. As engineering became more and more specialized (and this continues over the last thirty or forty years with computer engineering and biomedical engineering), the practice of academic engineering became more and more fixed in a collection of theories, models, and applications of those theories and models to build things and processes (engineering artifacts) and less focused on the *telos* of engineered products, and whether they are truly good for humankind in order to meet needs and relieve human suffering. Indeed, many new engineered articles being designed and created in the most developed countries of the world are often at the service of efficiency, corporate profit, human comfort and pleasure. It is therefore quite reasonable to ask whether engineering, as currently practiced in the developed world, is truly at the service of universal human goods and needs, or not.

What exactly do philosophy and theology have to say to engineering and its practice? Certainly, one can reasonably argue that designing and creating engineered products and materials that fulfill human wants, increase wealth, make the functioning of society more efficient, and improve the lives of persons are all good things Nonetheless, human ingenuity (the root of the word engineer) has enabled remarkably powerful discoveries and the application of these discoveries to the creation of new materials has led to human mastery of fission and the design and building of nuclear power plants for generating electricity. To the degree that this has led to carbon-neutral ways of generating electricity globally and the relieving of human misery by enabling, for example, refrigeration in countries in need of hospital care, medicines, and so forth, this is very good indeed. Conversely, the application of the knowledge of nuclear fission in creating nearly 70,000 nuclear warheads at the height of the Cold War,[3] and their proliferation to many countries of the world, has created a fear of catastrophic devastation that is indeed troublesome. A simple reflection on this one example reveals immediately that engineering and technology constitutes power in the hands of those who wield it, and can clearly be used for good or for ill.

So how do we ensure that engineers and the scientists who advance the disciplines that undergird engineering are sufficiently well formed and well educated to understand and to choose the good? I believe this relates strongly to one's presuppositions about the nature of truth, the relationship

3. Norris and Kristensen, "Global Nuclear Weapons Inventories."

among the disciplines and forms of knowledge, and the role of a university in addressing these issues.

The Nature of Truth

The university as we know it was born between the ninth and twelfth centuries in various parts of the world. The European university, the most immediate antecedent of what we know in the West, was born out of the medieval schools and in the heart of the Church. For example, the University of Paris emerged out of the cathedral school at Notre Dame de Paris in about 1150. These early universities were birthed in Christendom and so, of course, had a Christian worldview and our ultimate destiny in God. But even more importantly (perhaps), these early universities presupposed that truth or *veritas* is an objective, metaphysical reality that is rooted in "being." Being, the medievasl believed, is a reality that transcends sensate observation and that is ultimately the only reality that endures; i.e., spiritual or transcendent reality is "real" in the sense that it endures, while material reality is transitory. Indeed, God tells Moses, "I AM WHO I AM. This is what you are to say to the Israelites: 'I AM has sent me to you'" (Exod 3:14). God's very name is the personification of Being, and this Being is Truth.

Interestingly, modern science has helped us understand well how fleeting our material reality is. Specifically, Georges Lemaitre, the Belgian priest and physicist, helped us understand that the universe had an origin in the Big Bang.[4] Recently, physicists have predicted that the Universe is likely to either expand indefinitely into a "Big Freeze" or contract into a "Big Crunch," and that our own corner of the universe, the solar system, will cease to support life when the sun becomes a red giant and then collapses into a white dwarf. Thus, whatever human artifacts we generate on planet earth will not endure beyond the death of the solar system. However, the Being that supports all of that physical (and metaphysical) reality will endure. How do we know with some certitude that there must be non-sensate being that undergirds sensate reality? How do we know that physics must be complemented by metaphysics to have a complete view of the truth and of reality?

Without belaboring any proofs for the existence of an uncaused cause, or unmoved mover, or as Bernard Lonergan, the Jesuit philosopher, argues,

---

4. Lemaitre, "Beginning of the World."

an unconditioned reality,[5] we know that consciousness is not describable simply in terms of material neuronal interconnections (i.e. physiology and physics). An increasing number of documented near death experiences (NDEs) have resulted in out of body experiences (OBEs) in which the patient clearly describes events and objects that could only have been seen from outside the body.[6] Another pointer that metaphysical reality is worthy of investigation is attempting to explain why the universe appears to be of such extraordinarily low entropy—that is, highly improbable, the so called anthropic coincidences.[7] The argument some physicists have offered that this is no proof of a metaphysical reality is that there must be an infinity of universes (the multiverse) and we simply find ourselves in the one with this remarkably low entropy. One might reasonably ask which explanation is more incredible: that there is a non-sensate metaphysical, unconditioned reality (i.e., God) or that there are infinite universes, none of which we have any evidence of other than the one we reside in, which is so improbable. One could multiply other arguments, but suffice it to say that there are plenty of good reasons (from science and elsewhere) to explore seriously the possibility that a metaphysical unconditioned reality undergirds all of sensate reality, which is passing away. That is, *verum est ens.*

The Italian philosopher Giambattista Vico reformulated the classical formula *verum est ens* (truth is being) into a new reality: *verum quia factum*, that is, truth is whatever we have made ourselves. Vico rejected the notion that there is a spiritual or transcendental reality that supercedes and indeed is the source of truth. Here thereby introduced what Pope Emeritus Benedict has argued is the source of the modern mentality associated with truth; namely, that whatever humans make ourselves and whatever we can discover about what we have made (by performing historical analysis) is all we can know about truth. One can argue that this was the beginning of the dis-integration (literally) of the whole of education and of the liberal arts. Vico's formula was followed by Hegel's dialectic, by Comte's positivism, by Marx's *homo economicus*, and ultimately by the entire modern and post-modern infatuation with *factums*. At the root of the challenge associated with rejecting a metaphysics of any kind is the notion that truth and reality are reducible to purely material and sensate realities—that is, that everything that exists is simply the result of matter and physical processes.

5. See Lonergan, "Insight."

6. See, for example, Graden, *Near Death Experiences.*

7. See Spitzer, *New Proofs for the Existence of God*, s.v. "chapter two."

This inexorably leads to perhaps one of the greatest challenges of our age, namely the notion that *verum quia faciendum*: that truth is whatever we wish to make of it and that we can create our own world and our own truth. Indeed, you often hear scientists and engineers of the modern era make statements to the effect that whatever we can dream of in our minds, we can achieve. If truth can be reduced to whatever we wish to make of it, then engineers and technologists of the modern age come to believe that no matter how many unintended or undesirable consequences there may be to any given technology, we can always solve those challenges with more technology. A more enlightened view is to understand that the world we live in has an extraordinary treasure trove of creativity and diversity (there are at least an estimated 11–12 million living species of plants, animals, fungi, protists and bacteria on earth), and we should strive to retain that diversity to be a fantastic source of knowledge and resources.[8] This is the heritage that the Author of evolutionary biology has given us. Indeed, the work of insects, the most numerous animal species on earth, makes life livable for humans. Without insects, earth would quickly drown in detritus and become unlivable.

It is therefore important that the faculty of a university, no matter what discipline is their academic home, agree upon the origin of truth: the origin of truth generally, the origin of truth in their discipline, and how the truth of one discipline relates to another. In order to effect that understanding, it seems to me we need to probe the underlying philosophical framework of our disciplines and the methodological tools that we use.

THE PRESUPPOSITIONS THAT UNDERLIE SCIENCE AND ENGINEERING

Modern science was born in the seminal work of Francis Bacon, the Lord Chancellor of England, whose treatise *Novum Organum* entails the basis of the scientific method as a means of observation and induction. Clearly, one cannot build hypotheses, theories, and models, especially encompassed in mathematical elegance, unless what is being observed (nature) conforms to orderly laws. An essential presupposition of all of science is therefore that nature is orderly and obeys elegant and mathematically simple laws. That very naturally leads to the question: where do the laws of nature come from? Is there a *lawgiver*? Indeed, this question of the origin of nature's laws

8. Chapman, *Numbers of Living Species*, 1–80.

is one of the key considerations that led the atheist philosopher Antony Flew to recently change his worldview and confess a belief in God.[9]

Another essential presupposition of science and engineering is that the laws of nature are describable in elegant mathematical formulae. For example, the interconversion of matter and energy is describable by the equation E=mc2, a remarkably simple and elegant formula that captures the conversion of minute amounts of mass into enormous quantities of energy during nuclear fission. But why should it be that these laws of nature are expressible in such elegant mathematics? Why should the mathematics not be extremely complex? Or obey laws with fractional powers? That physics and other sciences should be guided by such elegance led Murray Gell-Mann, the Nobel Prize winning physics theorist to proclaim, "a chief criterion for the selection of a correct hypothesis . . . seems to be the criterion of beauty, simplicity, or elegance."[10] As with the origin of nature's laws, from whence comes this beauty and elegance? Who is the author of this beauty?

It seems to me that wrestling with these meta-questions, rather than evading them or simply stating that the presupposition of science is that there is no reality beyond matter (reductive materialism), is important for the future of science and for the integration of the disciplines. The presupposition of some scientists and all atheists that all reality is directly observable and sensible is incongruous with much of modern physics. Roughly forty years ago, cosmologists concluded that there must be some heretofore unobserved form of matter and energy if the rotational velocity of galaxies and the accelerating expansion of the universe were to be reconciled with known and observed forms of matter and energy. This led to the hypothesis, now widely subscribed to, that roughly 80 percent of the matter in the universe must be "dark matter," which is not observable, and roughly 68 percent of all energy must likewise be unobservable, or so-called "dark energy." These hypotheses have become part of the dogma of modern physics. But if scientists are able to subscribe to theories and hypotheses that entail belief in completely unobservable forms of matter and energy, then why do they struggle with openness to transcendence?

9. Flew, *There Is a God*.

10. Gell-Mann quoted in Johnson, *Strange Beauty*, 239.

THE TECHNOLOGICAL IMPERATIVE

Perhaps the biggest challenge to modern man, and to the university that helps to shape and form the mindset of us moderns, is that we can remake reality to our liking. As mentioned above, this is embodied in the statement *verum quia faciendum*, which is translated variously as "truth is whatever we make of it," or "truth is in the makeable," or more simply "it must be true." Clearly, there are limits to the truth that we can or should make. For example, the hubris implicit in the assumption that we can solve the challenges associated with anthropomorphic global warming through additional human interventions, such as cloud seeding, is troublesome. Understanding rather that the earth's climate, while it continues to change in response to both natural and manmade perturbations, is a delicate homeostasis with which we should strive to live in harmony seems like a concept that is worthy of careful consideration and deliberation.

Another notable example is that gender is simply a decision, rather than largely a biological reality. If we can remake our gender, then we can remake our genetic makeup to our liking and become a different species if we choose. This seems reminiscent of the remark made by 'the serpent' in the garden that God does not want us to eat the fruit from the tree in the center of the garden because "God knows that when you eat from it your eyes will be opened, and you will be like God, knowing good and evil" (Gen 3:5). The temptation to be like God is an old one and yet the reality of our existence is one rooted in billions of years of evolution, the unfolding of the universe, and the fact that our truth is grounded in Being.

THE ROLE OF THE UNIVERSITY

If the University is to truly be an institution that invites and integrates the disciplines to ask the ultimate questions, then technologists and engineers should openly and formally engage philosophers and theologians in the most important concepts that undergird our respective disciplines. Namely, what is the nature of truth? And how do results from modern physics, cosmology, biology, and other disciplines bear on the nature of reality? Is the truth about the world transcendent or not? Surely if it is, this must be one of the most important aspects of an education that we could provide those persons in our care.

Our students need to understand how they can approach these questions and develop the ability to formulate answers that are coherent, logical, and flow from thousands of years of asking. They would be foolish to attempt to do so without understanding well how the greatest thinkers in human history approached these questions. This involves understanding the forces that influence and change our culture and our approach to such questions.

We have attempted in this brief essay to examine the way in which humankind and culture have approached the nature of truth. This requires carefully asking the 'why' questions about those concepts which are assumed in our approach to acquiring and using new knowledge. Students must possess a framework or worldview and understand clearly the basis for their worldview in order to tackle the ultimate questions. It is the integration of the disciplines, not the fragmentation of those disciplines, that will enable our students a more fulsome understanding of their worldview.

As I mentioned above, I also believe that finding ways to bring the disciplines into dialogue will enable our students to better engage in civil and respectful dialogue. As our disciplines appear to grow farther apart, it seems our public discourse becomes shriller. I believe the two observations may be related. If one wants to understand one approach to engaging in civil, respectful discourse, I thoroughly endorse St. Thomas Aquinas's approach. No one has shown us a better method of both respecting and elevating our "opponents" views or of gracefully offering an alternative view.

St. Thomas, pray for us.

7

Forming Catholic Business Professionals Fit for Mission

CAROLYN Y. WOO

WHEN PONDERING NOTRE DAME'S invitation to lead the business college, the idea of leaving Purdue University was unthinkable. It is after all the institution that supported six of my seven years of study and which I had called home from my teens to my forties. My family was flourishing and our sons had grown into Boilermaker fans in the era of the "Three-peats": three consecutive Big Ten championships. For them, not showing up at those games bordered on betrayal.

My career could not be going better with committed mentors eager to teach me the ropes of higher education administration. Our Catholic faith meant a lot to my husband and me and we were still part of the campus parish where we first met when we served on the parish council. St. Thomas Aquinas Center was a large and vibrant community with strong adult catechesis programs and authentic commitment to social action. We did not believe that we needed to move to a Catholic campus to grow in our faith.

There was only one consideration that tugged at me: what does it mean to be a Catholic business school? I can be a Catholic at Purdue University but I cannot teach or promulgate the concept of Catholic Business there. While most academics at Catholic universities would readily offer that there is no Catholic Calculus, Catholic Physics, Catholic Chemistry, etc., I assert that there is Catholic Business.

BUSINESS: A NECESSARY GOOD

I have a deep affinity for business as I grew up in an immigrant family in Hong Kong where hundreds of thousands of families, like mine, re-settled after leaving everything behind in China to seek shelter first from the bombings in World War II and then to forge tenable futures for their children after the rise of the communist government. Hong Kong, with 426 square miles, could only offer its millions of people a deep harbor, a government that accepted the responsibility for the advancement of its citizens, and the Chinese "head for business." Commerce, not international aid, was the lifeline for the Hong Kong people.

One of my cousins from China started a small radio retail and repair store in a 100 square foot space nestled in the stair landing of a modest apartment building. With enterprise and learning, he contracted manufacturing for commonly used components. With time, this venture blossomed into a thriving export business.

Our family driver, Mr. Lai, a learned man who did his learning in Chinese, had to start from the bottom to "master" English which is the official language of the colony. We traded lessons: I tutored him in English and drilled him on pronunciation as we tried to untangle the sounds of "r" and "l." He got me ready for the Chinese portion of my grade six public examination that determined my standing for potential placement into the top-tier high schools.

Mr. Lai's English became good enough to be certified as a taxi driver. Hard work built up his savings that formed the down payment for his own taxi and a taxi license. Both the taxi and the license became financial assets that could be traded on the market. His homes mirrored his change in fortune: a lean-to of wood planks and corrugated tin roof gave way to one-room apartment with common bathroom and kitchen facilities in public housing, which the growing family eventually left for a condominium of three bedrooms. All three Lai children worked hard enough to earn their berths in the prestigious University of Hong Kong.

In my tenure at Catholic Relief Services, the importance of business to improving lives and eradicating poverty was profound. Aid is necessary at the onset of emergencies which leave large number of people without homes, money, livelihoods, food, medicines and destroy community infra-structures such as roads, bridges, schools, ports, utilities, etc. Yet aid is not meant to and cannot sustain the long-term well-being of communities. In addition to life-saving measures, recovery calls for supporting and estab-lishing local enterprises that could generate income for the people.

After typhoon Haiyan, with wind speeds as high as 195 mph that smashed into the islands of the Philippines, first responders moved into action, planning behind the scenes with a focus on mobilizing local busi-nesses. The intent was to make available to the beneficiaries cash (or electronic-cash more accurately) rather than supplies, so that they can pa-tronize local industries which in turn would generate employment. Since coconut trees, the main export from these islands, would take seven or more years to mature, solutions would required exploring other cash crops such as vegetables that can produce income fairly quickly. Analyses were undertaken to determine the amount of capital needed, sources for such investments, likely demand and potential buyers, pricing, costs and prob-able profits for the farmers.

One of my most enduring memories comes from a visit to Afghanistan where CRS programming sought to build the capacity of women through entrepreneurship. In this project, women learned the skills for small busi-ness start-ups and organized in groups of twenty to develop their business plans and put these into action. One group I visited produced butter cookies that smelled and tasted heavenly. CRS provided investment in the form of a wood burning oven and ingredients for an estimated three-month supply. When I spoke with the group, the members were ebullient. They had sold out all three months of cookies in one month. Their insatiable customers were the local police force whose consumption of these cookies resembles the donut run by police ubiquitous in American film and television.

With the help of a translator, I chatted with the leader as she was breast-feeding her baby. When I asked about her children, with sadness she replied that the first one had died of starvation because she could not produce enough milk to sustain him. The bakery now enabled her to feed both herself and her newborn. The benefit goes even further than liveli-hoods and survival. To achieve their goals, the women had to gain some degree of literacy in arithmetic, accounting, and governance. Education was addictive and they requested more training in business and in other areas of their lives: nutrition, health, savings, etc. They were able to afford the school fees for their children, including the girls. Their daughters who learned alongside them could imagine new ideas for and beyond their mothers' business. Husbands refrained from beating their wives who now earned income for the family. One overriding objective for the project was to create a source of cash other than poppies on which local farmers depended, and to achieve sufficient stability to counter the lure of extremist ideological groups which peddle hope in the face of hopelessness.

Discussions with potential private equity investors and the American owners of a farm in Nicaragua which grows mango, passion and dragon fruits were like a strategy session in a business school classroom. The farm had demonstrated success in exporting dried fruits and juice mixes to the juice bars which dot every street corner in the United States. Investment for expansion is needed to acquire more equipment located close to the fields, refrigerated trucks, production machinery and working capital for increased inventories and receivables. Its business potential notwithstanding, CRS did not move forward on the project as our priorities emphasize ownership by local communities and broader geographic engagement than this wonderful farm could offer. I left with my heart singing as I could see how business models like this one provide paths for market engagement and increase wealth for the farmers involved.

Social transformation in the western highlands of Guatemala requires livelihood plans and the acquisition of investment capital to drive large scale community advancement. This area of Guatemala is plagued with severe childhood malnutrition and endemic poverty which renders it a prime target for gang bullying and recruitment. CRS works with the local leaders of over two hundred communities to build their capacities for self-determination by creating livelihood strategies and corresponding business plans. Of a grant of fifty million US dollars, twenty-five went into training and education, while the other half was held as capital to support the resulting enterprises from the livelihood plans. This capital would be allocated as interest-free loans to be repaid so that the pool could support other startups. As part of CRS's deliverables, the agency would raise an additional fund of fifty million US dollars from private investors as they now could assess the track record and potential of these enterprises after they have passed through the start-up or highest risk stage.

On a macro level, we have seen that direct foreign investments, market economies and participation in the global economy can increase prosperity. Benefits to citizens include employment, job training, higher standards of living, and savings. Economic activities also promulgate infrastructures for roads, ports, rail, information systems, monetary policies, regulatory frameworks, education and financial institutions. Multinationals with operations in developing countries can set requirements for revenue distribution and reporting protocol that promote transparency and multi-lateral collaboration between local governments, non- governmental organizations and transnational agencies such as development banks, the International Monetary Fund and the World Bank. Considering that the three primary causes of conflict are corruption, poverty, and extreme inequality, it is not difficult to see that commerce can enhance peace.

These benefits have triggered the emergence and growth of impact investing. The latter entails the use of private investments, beyond philanthropy and government capital, to address large scale social problems. Investment is directed to social enterprises that could provide much needed services to the poor at rates they could afford while delivering a return to the providers of capital. Fee for services is a sustainable model while free service is not. Impact investing has been applied to needs such as the provision of water, health services, seeds, education, insurance for unpredictable weather events, waste removal, affordable housing, working capital for farmers, and more.

In 2014 and 2016, CRS worked with the Vatican Pontifical Council for Justice and Peace to host two conferences which explored the proper use of impact investing. At the end of the 2014 Conference, Pope Francis concluded,

> A sense of solidarity with the poor and with the marginalized has led you to reflect on impact investing as one emerging form of responsible investment. Representatives of the Roman Curia have joined you in these days of study aimed at assessing innovative forms of investment which can benefit local communities and the environment, as well as providing a reasonable return. Impact investors are those who are conscious of the existence of serious unjust situations, instances of profound social inequality and unacceptable conditions of poverty affecting communities and entire peoples. These investors turn to financial institutes which will use their resources to promote the economic and social development of these groups through investment funds aimed at satisfying basic needs associated with agriculture, access to water, adequate

housing and reasonable prices, as well as with primary health care and educational services.[1]

All the above examples notwithstanding, it is safe to say that the potential of business for good is far from being realized. Daily scandals in the media point out fraudulent banking practices, overpriced medication, aggressive marketing of harmful products, inappropriate outreach to children, inappropriate and even illegal transfer of personal data, exploitation of labor and local communities, and falsification of test results pertaining to compliance with regulatory standards. On a macro level, average inflation-adjusted income of households in the US and many developed countries have not risen for almost two decades. Prosperity favors an alarmingly thin slice of individuals at the very top of the pyramid. Pope Francis, in *Laudato si'*, decries the destruction of the environment, our common home, by our unlimited consumption of goods and penchant for waste.

CATHOLIC BUSINESS

Beginning with Pope Leo XIII in 1891, a tradition of reflections, letters and encyclicals have promulgated the social teachings of the Church, which depict an unambiguous vision for the roles of business and markets. Catholic Social Teaching asserts that the purpose of business must be to enable human flourishing for all, particularly the poorest, most marginalized and vulnerable. Unacceptable are the oppression of people without power, and unbridled greed that subjugate people to profits.

Pope Paul VI, in *Populorum Progressio* warned against "unbridled liberalism" when,

> certain concepts have somehow . . . insinuated themselves into the fabric of human society. These concepts present profit as the chief spur to economic progress, free competition as the guiding norm of economics, and private ownership of the means of production as an absolute right, having no limits nor concomitant social obligations. This unbridled liberalism paves the way for a particular type of tyranny, rightly condemned by our predecessor Pius XI, for it results in the "international imperialism of money." Such improper manipulations of economic forces can never be

---

1. Francis, "To Participants."

condemned enough; let it be said once again that economics is supposed to be in the service of man.[2]

Continuing this line of teaching in *Centesimus Annus*, Saint Pope John Paul II states, "In fact, the purpose of a business firm is not simply to make a profit, but is to be found in its very existence as a community of persons who in various ways are endeavoring to satisfy their basic needs, and who form a particular group at the service of the whole of society."[3]

In *Caritas in Veritate*, Pope Benedict XVI situates the foundation of all exchanges, including those of an economic nature, in the concept of gift. The Christian precept is that our activities result from the giving to and taking from God who is the source of all gifts. All exchanges are expressions of gratuity for the benefit of each other. Thus, "commercial entities based on mutualist principles and pursuing social ends . . . types of economic initiative which, without rejecting profit, aim at a higher goal than the mere logic of the exchange of equivalents, of profit as an end in itself," but instead "view profit as a means of achieving the goal of a more humane market and society."[4]

Pope Francis connects the unrestrained pursuit of profit, growth and consumption to the bankruptcy of our environment which he reminds us is a gift from God as our common home for our life together. He instructs in *Laudato si'*,

> Where profits alone count, there can be no thinking about the rhythms of nature, its phases of decay and regeneration, or the complexity of ecosystems which may be gravely upset by human intervention. Moreover, biodiversity is considered at most a deposit of economic resources available for exploitation, with no serious thought for the real value of things, their significance for persons and cultures, or the concerns and needs of the poor.[5]

Catholic Business does not call for the rejection of business and even profits. Our tradition recognizes the benefits of exchanges as ways to meet each other's needs as well as the role of enterprise for creating enriching employment and developing human potential. But it calls for conduct governed by the responsibilities to honor the dignity of individuals, advance

2. Paul VI, "Populorum Progressio," par. 26.

3. John Paul II, "Centesimus Annus," par. 35.

4. Benedict XVI, "Caritas in Veritate," par. 38, 46.

5. Francis, "Laudato Si," par. 190.

the good of all, enable self-determination by the people affected through proper delegation, and safeguard the environment for the nourishing of all: rich and poor, current and future generations.

FORMATION OF THE CATHOLIC BUSINESS PROFESSIONAL

Whatever the failures of business are, one can safely conclude that these are the failures of the people who comprise these enterprises. As Pope Benedict clearly stated in *Caritas in Veritate*, the market "cannot rely on itself, because it is not able to produce by itself something that lies outside its competence. It must draw its moral energies from other subjects that are capable of generating them."[6] He goes further to state,

> The Church has always held that economic action is not to be regarded as something opposed to society. . . . Admitted, the market can be a negative force, not because it is so by nature, but because a certain ideology can make it so. . . . But it is man's darkened reason that produces these consequences, not the instrument per se. Therefore it is not the instrument that must be called to account, but individuals, their moral conscience and their personal and social responsibility.[7]

While business schools impart standard methodologies for students to determine the future value of money, calibrate risks of all kinds, or search for optimal solutions given objectives and constraints, these are merely tools to assist in the achievement of vision. Unfortunately, the social contract of business with society tends to be the question shielded from debate in business school curricula. Its place is filled by the unquestioned assertion that the purpose of business is to maximize the wealth of shareholders or the owners of the firm. This assumption is at best stifling, suffocating, and insulting to business students with the implicit assumption that they do not care for the good of others. At worst, such orientation is idolatrous.

Catholic Business, standing on the foundations of Catholic Social Teaching, rejects the primacy of profits and raises up the vistas of human well-being, dignity of the individual, care of creation and service to the common good as destinations worthy of those who see themselves as

6. Benedict XVI, "Caritas in Veritate," par. 35.

7. Benedict XVI, "Caritas in Veritate," par. 36.

created by God to bring about his kingdom. Business is an inherently human enterprise constituted by the intentional exchanges that people undertake for their mutual benefits. Scripture reminds us that our actions are either for God or against God (see, e.g., Matt 6:24). The myriad decisions every business person makes, from the mundane to the dramatic, can be the holy ground where we serve God in the other, may they be customers, clients, colleagues, capital providers, suppliers and neighbors. Catholic Business mandates that we prepare students to recognize, seek and stand in this holy ground.

How do we form students for the above vocation? Almost all business schools host some type of ethics courses to give attention to legal breaches, raise awareness for where lines are blurred, introduce frameworks for assessing ethical trade-offs between options, delineate laws and penalties, or showcase systems for training and compliance. Much of the focus is on the distinction between right and wrong and the tangible consequences of the latter. Yet the formation needed is not so much teaching students right from wrong: they already know. Decades of research in moral agency and personal efficacy demonstrate that knowing does not lead to doing. All forms of rationalization lead one to avoid responsibility, whitewash consequences, or settle for laudable ends over dubious means.

Catholic Business must enable our students to situate their choices in the desire for good, and fundamentally, the desire for God. But our students cannot love deeply what they do not know. This is the basis behind our earliest catechism lesson that the purpose for a Christian is to "know God, love God and serve God." This sequence is not accidental. While God cannot be contained by human imagination, God seeks to be known.

JOHN CAVADINI AS MENTOR AND PARTNER

This is a tall order and here I must state my debt to John Cavadini for making this endeavor possible, and I dare say, even probable. Cavadini has helped shape Notre Dame as a place where the revelation of God in Christ through the Holy Spirit is approached with intellectual seriousness. The meditation on that revelation constitutes theology, which gives context to and fructifies students' work in other disciplines. During his watch, it was popular for students to seek a double major or minor in theology. Theology, under Cavadini, wasn't intellectual window-dressing, nor did it become captured by social activism (however important this might be) at the expense of rigorous reflection on Christian revelation.

John's vision for theology to be a point of transcendence and integration of other disciplines is essential to formation where faith, wholeness and transcendence are to constitute the touchstone for students. In his own words,

> Having a theology department means accepting a commitment to the intellectual life as oriented toward an "understanding" of something that integrates and transcends all disciplines. Such an understanding keeps each discipline from closing in on itself and proceeding as if the truths it discovers were incommensurable with the truths discovered by other disciplines. It means openness to a conversation that necessarily transcends each discipline but is not merely "interdisciplinary." If the disciplines converge at some point, it must be at a point "above" them all, in a discipline that has as its explicit object of study the mystery that transcends all other objects of study.[8]

Ironically, Cavadini's understanding of transcendence inherent in the study of theology does not denote a haughty and elitist stance over other disciplines. On the contrary, he exhibits a humility and collegiality in the way he defers to the knowledge and truth that is the purview of the other disciplines, like business, for example. I appreciate Cavadini's reaching out to me on the premise that business school is a fertile and necessary partner for the formation of future business professionals fit for bringing about God's kingdom. Cavadini does not castigate business as a necessary evil which narrows and corrupts students. Rather, he sees the potential of business for good and recognizes that effective service requires strong administrative acumen. For this, he encouraged joint courses such as The Character Project and workshops to enhance the success of Catholic university presidents, seminarians, youth ministers, leaders of social service agencies, and publishers, among others.

Intellectualizing faith can be a hazard of institutions that glorify the life of the mind. Values are not just cultivated in a vacuum or simply in the mind. They take hold as we see others in action which strengthens our own agency. Engagement of the people at the periphery or at the bottom of society allows students to come in touch with others' suffering, and reflect on the causes and their complicity in the systems from which they benefit.

8. Cavadini, "Why Study God?"

Cavadini has consistently championed the pastoral and service dimensions of study at a Catholic university as essential to helping students see, judge, and act. Among many other ways, our partnership over the years has produced much fruit from that commitment.

In reflection, my partnership with Cavadini is quite unexpected and amusing: a business school dean with a theology department chair; a theological neophyte and a master of St. Augustine and the Church Fathers; a seeming pragmatist and a seeming idealist. This must be the humor and the providence of God. Without Cavadini, I would know the destination but not have had the road map nor tools for the formation of Catholic Business professionals. The theology curricula under Cavadini challenged and equipped our students to grow into an adult faith that can name the world's blindness while encouraging them not to be afraid of that world—for it's the very world that the students must enter and in which they must serve. His grounding provides students a background of meaning, transcendence, and commitment that contextualizes their professional pursuits.

The particular contribution and brilliance of Cavadini is that he labors not to speak generically about "meaning," "purpose," "mission," but to see each of these as following from the gift of revelation, the study of which he and the whole Department of Theology bear responsibility. He knows deeply that when students have been guided to know the God of Christianity, the humble God, the "downwardly mobile" God, then the Catholic university has done its job, for knowledge of this God will explode out into other spheres of their lives and work. Thus, he helps his fellow colleagues in the faculty and administration to ready students who will be able to name evil systems, ambitions, and temptations in the world by comparing them with the absolute humility of incarnate love. This is the mature and enduring faith that Notre Dame enables in our students to go forth confidently with a burning desire and ability to name what is true, good, and beautiful in the wider world, and that which is not.

8

The Challenge of "Scientific Atheism"

Stephen M. Barr

THE CURRENT SITUATION

I HAVE HAD THE opportunity to speak with many hundreds of Catholics about science and religion over the last twenty years: in private conversations, by e-mail, and in Q&A sessions after public lectures I have given. I have come to realize how much unsettlement, nervousness, and even fear there is among Catholics about the relation of reason and faith.

Theoretically, there shouldn't be. A believing Catholic shouldn't think that scientific truth could contradict the truths of the faith. As *Gaudium et Spes* put it, "Methodical research in all branches of knowledge, provided it is carried out in a truly scientific manner . . . can never conflict with the faith, because the things of the world and the things of faith derive from the same God."[1]

And yet anxiety there is.

There are many reasons for it. Atheist scientists, such as Richard Dawkins, Steven Weinberg, Stephen Hawking, Victor Stenger, and Lawrence Krauss, have been very vocal. They get a great deal of media attention, and this reinforces the widespread impression that the scientific community

1. Flannery, "Gaudium et Spes," par. 36.

is devoid of religious faith. The historical myth that modern science and religion have always been at war, although completely discredited among historians, is the conventional wisdom among educated and uneducated people alike. When I ask Catholic audiences what name comes to mind when they think about the Church's relation to science, they immediately and in one voice reply, "Galileo!"

People have been told that faith is believing without evidence, whereas science is all about evidence. The false idea that faith is a blind leap has become a cliché. Belief in miracles has come to be seen as unscientific, almost as a matter of definition. The accounts in the Book of Genesis don't seem to match up with what science has learned; and all that many lay people are told about this is that the Book of Genesis isn't to be taken too literally. But how it *should* be taken, they are rarely told.

I think many Catholics live in fear—and almost the expectation—that any day there is likely to be a scientific discovery that will overturn the religious applecart. They read that the great Stephen Hawking has said that the universe can create itself by a quantum fluctuation. They hear that a magical thing called "the God particle" has been discovered and they imagine it must do something that God was once thought to do. They are told that computers will someday achieve consciousness and be more intelligent than human beings. They read that neuroscience is disproving the reality of free will and the soul. And they worry what the discovery of extraterrestrial life would mean.

In short, modern science is looked upon as theologically threatening. And it has most definitely created intellectual difficulties for many believers. According to recent studies, a perception that science and religion are incompatible is a significant factor in Catholics losing their faith. Clearly, this is an enormous pastoral problem for the Catholic Church.

The good news is that in recent years, especially in the United States, many creative initiatives have begun to address this problem. These efforts, often started independently and without knowledge of each other, have begun to connect and cooperate. A key figure in these developments has been Dr. John Cavadini, who was among the first to grasp the seriousness of the problem and to have the energy and vision to do something about it. He organized conferences for bishops, priests, and young Catholic theologians to help inform them on these issues and equip them to meet the challenge. He began a program of week-long summer seminars at the University of Notre Dame for teachers of biology, physics, chemistry, and religion in Catholic high schools to prepare them to set up programs on science and religion in their own schools. (This program is now working jointly with a similar one started independently in New Orleans by Dr. Christopher T. Baglow, who has himself since moved to join Cavadini's institute at Notre Dame.) The McGrath Institute for Church Life, at Cavadini's instigation, has promoted and supported a variety of other efforts, including giving vital assistance to the Society of Catholic Scientists, which was formed in 2016.

THE ROOTS OF THE PROBLEM

While the problem seems to have grown more acute in recent decades, it has been gathering force for centuries, indeed from the very beginnings of modern science. Historians point to a number of philosophical shocks produced by the Scientific Revolution of the sixteenth and seventeenth centuries.

One of these was the unravelling of the medieval intellectual synthesis. In the Middle Ages, Aristotelianism became the language of both theology and science. But modern science began to develop its own very different vocabulary, and the two worlds gradually drifted apart and stopped talking to each other. Theology and science were not enemies, but they did become strangers.

A second shock was the abandonment of teleology in favor of mechanistic explanations, especially in the physical sciences. This was, of course, one of the things that helped destroy the Aristotelian synthesis.

A third shock was the determinism of the laws discovered by Newton and indeed of all of the laws of classical physics. This determinism created an enormous problem for belief in human free will and (especially for Protestant theologians) a question of how even God could act freely in the world.

Finally, the success of the reductive methods of modern science, whereby the properties and behavior of things are understood in terms of the interactions of their constituent parts, tended to inspire a variety of reductive philosophical ideas, including the materialism and scientism that have become such formidable threats to faith today.

It is understandable that some people think modern science itself is to blame for all of this. They don't see how its rise and development could have led to all these baneful consequences for faith if modern science weren't itself defective in some way. One finds this stated or implied in much Catholic discourse about modern science and the Scientific Revolution that gave birth to it.

Declinism in various forms is popular with some Catholic thinkers. By this I mean the tendency to trace all modern ills to some intellectual mistake, sometimes rather subtle, in the distant past that caused the train of history to go off the rails, leading to a succession of nearly inevitable and worsening disasters: the Reformation, the Enlightenment, and the rise of various pernicious modern ideologies. Sometimes the trail of error is traced back to William of Ockham or sometimes even further. I am not denying that there is some truth in these stories, but clearly this tendency can be taken too far.

A similar story is often told by Catholic intellectuals about modern science. Here the culprits are usually identified as Francis Bacon and René Descartes, with sometimes Galileo and Hobbes mentioned as accomplices. According to these accounts, modern science was conceived in philosophical error, and thereby its nature was corrupted and its vision distorted from the very beginning. The materialism and scientism which plague us today are seen as simply the logical outcome of modern science's flawed philosophical foundations.

There are at least four ways in which modern science and its methods are seen by some Catholic commentators as flawed and as giving us a distorted picture of nature:

First, it is said, modern science was motivated chiefly by a desire to dominate nature and control it for our own purposes, rather than by a desire to know the truth of things and their natural ends. Not *episteme*, but *techne* was the prized goal. One contemporary writer puts this view very clearly: "For ancient philosophers, the dignity of contemplation lay in its fulfillment of our longing for truth. The architects of modern thought [Bacon, Descartes, Galileo, and Hobbes] championed analysis for the sake of ever-greater power and security."[2]

Often quoted is Descartes's statement that science will allow us to become the "masters and possessors of nature."[3] Also frequently cited is the statement attributed to Francis Bacon that we should "torture nature's secrets from her." These statements and others like them are also popular

2. Shiffman, "Humanity 4.5."

3. Descartes, *Discourse on Method and Meditations*, 35.

with feminist historians of science, who take these as evidence that Western science is phallocratic, dominating and destructive. Here it should be said in Bacon's defense that his statement about torturing nature for answers had nothing to do with sadism, domination or lack of respect for the created world. He was merely advocating, using a memorable metaphor, the need for "doing experiments." And the need for experimentation in science most definitely needed advocates at that time, because the view of Aristotelians was that man-made devices, including those used to perform experiments, did not teach one about nature, since they forced things to move in a violent or artificial way rather than according to their natural motion.

A second criticism of modern science is that it willfully blinded itself to formal and final causes, allowing only material and efficient causes into scientific explanation. This criticism is so common and well known that it is not necessary for me to document it here. But still, I think it useful to quote two statements by prominent Catholic thinkers. The first statement, by a well-known Catholic theologian, is the following: "Modern science first excludes *a priori* final and formal causes, then investigates nature under the reductive mode of mechanism (efficient and material causes), and then turns around to claim both final and formal causes are obviously unreal, and also that its [own] mode of knowing the corporeal world takes priority over all other forms of human knowledge."[4]

Note something very significant. This author is simply equating "modern science" with scientism. The assertions that things not discussed by science are unreal and that science always has priority over other ways of knowing are obviously statements *about* science—meta-scientific statements—not statements *of* science. Many scientists might endorse them, but I daresay far more would reject them. What I think is revealing about this quote is how easily and unconsciously its author attributes the errors of scientism to modern science as such.

The second quote is from an article by the late Cardinal Dulles, who is describing with evident approval the views of Etienne Gilson:

> The Thomist philosopher Etienne Gilson vigorously contended in his 1971 book *From Aristotle to Darwin and Back Again* that Francis Bacon and others perpetrated a *philosophical error* when they eliminated two of Aristotle's four causes from *the purview of science*. They sought to explain everything in mechanistic terms,

4. Schönborn, "Designs of Science."

referring only to material and efficient causes and discarding formal and final causality.[5]

It is a philosophical error to deny the *reality* of final and formal causes. And Bacon and others may well have committed it. But what they are accused of by Gilson, according to Dulles, is merely saying that such causes shouldn't be within "the purview of science." That is not the same thing. And to equate the two things is, again, to confuse a certain view about how science should be conducted (which Dulles clearly considers to be part of how modern science has defined itself since Bacon), with certain radical philosophical claims. Again, we see the implicit attribution of philosophical error to modern science as such.

A third accusation leveled against modern science is that it regards itself as being only about appearances and phenomena rather than the reality underlying those appearances or the unseen causes of those phenomena. In other words, modern science is accused of being inherently positivistic in its self-understanding. In the words of the well-known theologian quoted earlier, "physical reality is conceived of according to the reductive claims of modern science (which is to say, positivism)."[6] Note again, the simple identification of modern science with radical philosophical positions. Science does not just employ reductive methods; science as such makes reductive *claims*. And those claims are said to be positivistic.

There is a paradoxical aspect to the way some Catholic authors discuss modern science. They castigate positivism and claim to be champions of a realist view of science—realism being the view that science tells one about reality. And yet one sometimes finds the very same authors making positivistic statements about modern science themselves. In particular, one finds them saying that modern science is only about fitting the data, making quantitative predictions, and controlling nature. They say that the theories of modern science are always provisional and approximate and therefore not the truth about nature, but just models that work. The highly mathematical entities posited by modern science are said to be merely *entia rationis*, mental constructs that are useful in correlating measured quantities, but which correspond to no entities outside the mind.

This is connected to a fourth critique of modern science, which is that by confining itself to the measurable and the quantitative, it can deal only with relatively superficial aspects of reality. Much of this critique comes

5. Dulles, "God and Evolution."
6. Schönborn, "Designs of Science."

from an Aristotelian perspective, according to which quantity pertains primarily to adventitious accidental features of things, such as location, size, and so on, rather than to their natures, essences and causes. Whether a cat is here or there, is moving or at rest, is large or small, is in this or that spatial configuration (such as sitting or standing), or whether it is one of a large or small number of cats, makes no difference to what a cat is or to its essential properties. What is gained in precision and rigor by the quantitative methods of modern science is lost in ontological depth, so to speak.

Of course, there is some truth in all of these claims. The control of nature for our benefit and practical applications are a very large part of modern science. An exclusive focus on mechanisms can make one lose sight of teleology. Positivism has indeed left a residue in the thinking of many scientists. And there is much about reality—including the most important things—that cannot be explained by the quantitative sciences, such as physics.

Yet, on the whole, the conventional critique of modern science that I have sketched above is very wide of the mark.

AN UNHELPFUL CRITIQUE AND CARICATURE OF MODERN SCIENCE

The critique of modern science that I just outlined is misguided and unhelpful, I believe, for several reasons. First, it is largely based on a caricature of modern science. Second, it leads much of Catholic commentary on modern science to have a defensive, fearful, and even hostile tone, which interferes with the task of evangelizing a world that rightly esteems the achievements of science and that is increasingly influenced by scientific modes of thought. And third, it leads to misdiagnoses that mistake friends for enemies and enemies for friends, and causes some Catholics to embrace ideas that are actually corrosive to traditional faith and to resist ideas that are actually apologetically helpful.

I cannot adequately support all of these contentions in an article of reasonable length, especially as I wish to spend the last part of it delivering a more positive message. I will only briefly discuss my reasons for making them, beginning with the idea that the chief inspiration of modern science is the desire to control and manipulate nature for our own purposes rather than to know truth for its own sake. I will answer this first by quoting some statements made by St. John Paul II in an address to the Pontifical Academy of Science on November 10, 1979, at a commemoration of the centenary of the birth of Albert Einstein. He said,

> The search for truth is the task of basic science. The researcher who moves on this first level of science, feels all the fascination of St. Augustine's words: "*Intellectum valde ama*," "greatly love understanding!" and the function that is characteristic of it, to know truth. Pure science is a good. . . . On its second level [*versant*], science turns to practical applications, which find their full development in the various technologies. In the phase of its concrete achievements, science is necessary to mankind to satisfy the rightful requirements of life, and to overcome the different ills that threaten it. There is no doubt that applied science has rendered and will continue to render immense services to man, provided it is inspired by love, regulated by wisdom, and accompanied by the courage that defends it against the undue interference of all tyrannical powers.[7]

Note the very positive assessment of science, both in its pure and applied forms. But note also that St. John Paul II placed the search for truth as the first level of science. Indeed, that search is what does motivate most scientists. They do "love understanding."

What is it that fires the imagination of most young people when first attracted to science? It is the marvels of nature: dinosaurs, weird creatures from the ocean depths, the Big Bang, black holes, amazingly beautiful pictures from the Hubble Space Telescope of colorful planets and moons and awe-inspiring galaxies and nebulas—things that are completely useless to know about from a practical point of view. What stirs the soul of most scientists and science lovers is the thrill of discovery. It is the excitement of Archimedes's exclamation "Eureka!" Yes, Archimedes had hit upon the solution of a practical problem, how to determine whether the King's crown was made of pure gold; but what undoubtedly excited Archimedes much more was that he had gained a sudden insight into nature.

As St. Augustine understood, the thirst for understanding is a thirst for God. Let us remember the words of Johannes Kepler, when he made perhaps the first great discovery of modern science. He wrote, "I thank thee, Lord God our Creator, that thou hast allowed me to see the beauty in thy work of creation." To tell people who love or respect science that it's

7. John Paul II, "Deep Harmony," par. 2–3.

primarily about domination and control is to do them an injustice and to invite their scorn.

I turn now to the question of final and formal causes and their supposed banishment from modern science. I say "supposed banishment," because I believe final and formal causality are still very much a part of modern science. What were banished—or rather set aside—were certain Aristotelian ways of thinking about these things. And there was a reason they were set aside: they had proven scientifically sterile, at least in physics, astronomy, and the areas where modern science was to score its first great triumphs.

Let me quote from a recent book by Dr. Jude Dougherty of the Catholic University of America:

> Modern science in the sixteenth and seventeenth centuries rightly shifted its interest to mechanistic explanations of natural phenomena, limiting explanation to efficient and material causes. It must be acknowledged that the endeavor to explain sensible things in the light of their substantial form or telos was a stumbling block for the Peripatetic tradition for centuries. Its sterile attempts were quickly outmoded by the quantitative procedures of modern physics and chemistry. Today we would say that there is no point in asking the purpose of limestone deposits in Indiana or that of penguins in the Antarctic.[8]

This very clear-eyed appraisal was written by a philosopher who is no enemy of teleology, but indeed a foremost champion of Aristotelian-Thomistic thought in our time.

Or listen to Fr. Stanley Jaki, also no enemy of Aristotle or St. Thomas, in his book *The Road of Science and the Ways to God*: "Bacon therefore could and did banish from physics the study of final causes as barren virgins, and he rightly insisted on the disastrous effect of their study in the physics of Aristotle."[9] Nevertheless, as Fr. Jaki also emphasized, the scientists of the seventeenth century were by no means opposed to the idea of purpose in nature. Quite the contrary. He says, "On one crucial point Bacon was not the guide of Hooke and his associates in the Royal Society. Their works were a continual celebration of purposeful arrangements in nature."[10] Jaki then spends several pages describing the enthusiastic embrace of teleology

8. Dougherty, *Nature of Scientific Explanation*, 60.

9. Jaki, *Road of Science*, 53.

10. Jaki, *Road of Science*, 80.

by Robert Hooke, Nehemiah Grew, Robert Boyle, William Harvey, Isaac Newton, and other leading British scientists of the time.

The point is that the scientists of the seventeenth century were not opposed to the idea of purpose in nature; they simply thought that it didn't help one understand the operations of nature—that is, how it works. Modern scientists do indeed search for physical "mechanisms" to explain phenomena. But as the late Dr. Austin L. Hughes, a Catholic evolutionary biologist, noted in his brilliant (but still unpublished) book *The Folly of Scientism*, the very idea of a physical "mechanism" is based on an analogy between natural processes and machines. And the only actual machines that we know about are ones built by human beings for a purpose. Thus, mechanism does not exclude purpose, but can go hand in hand with it. As Hughes further noted, however, once a machine is built by a human being it generally "goes about its business without regard for our expectations." In other words, to understand the operation of a machine, how it does what it does, one need not advert to the purposes of the one who built it. Hughes spoke of modern science as involving a form of "ascesis" or self-denial. He wrote, "The scientific method involves deliberately setting aside certain ways of thinking to which our minds naturally tend. . . . The great discovery of modern science is that we can learn a lot about nature by this kind of self-denial."[11]

At this point, many Aristotelian-Thomist philosophers would likely point out that the purposiveness of machines is very different from the finality one finds in natural kinds, such as animals and plants. The machine is built "for the sake of" something or someone other than itself—the automobile is for the sake of the driver, for example. By contrast, the activity of a plant or animal is for the sake of its own flourishing, the perfecting or realizing of its own nature. Modern science, however, is not blind to this kind of purposiveness, though some people imagine that it is. For example, consider the following statement of Cardinal Dulles, from the same article I quoted above. After saying that modern science has "discarded" final causes, he explains why this is a mistake: "Final causality is particularly important in the realm of living organisms. The organs of the animal or human body are not intelligible except in terms of their purpose or finality. The brain is not intelligible without reference to the faculty of thinking that

11. Hughes, *Folly of Scientism*.

is its purpose, nor is the eye intelligible without reference to the function of seeing."[12]

The fact, however, is that modern science is not oblivious to the fact that the function of an eye is to see and of the brain is to think, or that the function of the immune system is immunity, of the respiratory system respiration, of the reproductive system reproduction, of the visual cortex vision, and so on. That indeed is why scientists name them as they do. And scientists well understand that these functions are ordered to the flourishing of these creatures.

But doesn't Darwinian evolution deny teleology? Yes and no. It certainly does as regards the mutations that fuel evolutionary change. These are said not to be aiming at anything, to be undirected toward a goal. The mutations happen willy-nilly, quite apart from whether they are beneficial or harmful. There is a teleology, however, not always noticed or acknowledged, in Darwinian evolution. It is to be found in the process of natural selection.

Why does natural selection favor this mutation but not that one? Because this one makes the eye see better in some way, which serves the *purpose of* helping the creature find food or mates or avoid predators, which in turn serves the *purpose* of helping the animal to live and thrive and reproduce. Why, on the other hand, do species that take up residence in dark caves often gradually become blind and even sometimes lose their eyes? Because seeing serves no *purpose* for them, and so mutations that harm the faculty of sight are not selected against. It is mutations that confer a benefit—an advantage—that get fixed in the population by selection. Teleology thus enters at the back door, as it were; but enter it does. Darwinism can account for very little indeed without bringing intrinsic finality into its explanation. Indeed, the famous evolutionary biologist Ernst Mayr admitted that finalistic explanations play an important role in evolution, though he chose to call them "teleonomic" rather than teleological.[13] But, as Stanley Jaki noted, that is a distinction without much difference.[14]

Admittedly, a modern biologist who is an atheist would not say there are goals or ends in biology in the sense of purposes in the mind of a Creator God, but neither, for that matter, would Aristotle have said that. It is also wrong to think that modern science has no use for formal causes. It

12. Dulles, "God and Evolution."

13. Mayr, "Teleological and Teleonomic," 91–117.

14. Jaki, *Road of Science*, 294.

appeals to form all the time. For example, a liver and a muscle are made up of the same material constituents—hydrogen, carbon, oxygen, and so on—acting on each other by the same basic forces. It is precisely their *forms,* in the sense of the way the matter is organized, their organic structures, that differ and enable them to play different roles in the body.

The same is true in physics. The very same carbon atoms can form a diamond, which is transparent, hard, and electrically insulating, or they can form a piece of graphite, which is opaque, soft, and electrically conducting. What explains their different properties is the difference in *form,* in intelligible structure. Indeed, as one goes deeper into fundamental physics, one finds that matter itself seems almost to dissolve into the pure forms of advanced mathematics.

The question is not whether form is important in modern science; it is whether the forms of modern physics and biology—namely *structure* of various types—corresponds to the Aristotelian notion of substantial form. There is at least some similarity. An Aristotelian philosopher who recognizes this is Jude Dougherty. He considers this question at length in *The Nature of Scientific Explanation.* After discussing the role of structure in modern science he says, "Permit me to make a distinction, lest it be supposed that I have been identifying structure with the Aristotelian concept of essence. Structure is not a synonym for essence. Structure is in the order of accident; . . . This is not to say that structure does not explain a great deal. If we know the structure of a molecule or organism, we can make a great many predictions about it."[15] He goes on to explain that structure is "in the order of accident" partly because the structure of things can be modified without changing them essentially. But then he notes that structural changes can also change things from one kind to another and concludes that not all structure is accidental: "There seems to be a distinction between essential structure and accidental structure."[16] This leads him to ask, rhetorically, "Have we reached the point where we are willing to say that the structures postulated by or described by the sciences are really nothing other than Aristotle's forms?"[17]

In the end, he rejects that conclusion. But his discussion shows an appreciation of the fact that central to modern science and its explanations are notions of form—in fact, enormously rich and fruitful notions

15. Dougherty, *Nature of Scientific Explanation,* 41–42.
16. Dougherty, *Nature of Scientific Explanation,* 42–43.
17. Dougherty, *Nature of Scientific Explanation,* 43.

of form—and these forms bear some resemblance to those of Aristotelian philosophy, even if they may not be quite the same. The notion that formal causality has been banished from modern science is at best a gross oversimplification, but in my view actually the reverse of the truth.

I now turn to the accusation that modern science is positivistic. The heyday of positivism was the first half of the twentieth century, when it was extremely influential, perhaps dominant, among philosophers of science and also affected the thinking of many scientists. Einstein in developing his theory of gravity (General Relativity) was influenced by the ideas of Ernst Mach, who was one of the founders of positivism. And as physicists tried to make sense of quantum mechanics in the 1920s and 1930s, they often resorted to positivist ideas or ways of speaking. The reason they did is the following: in thinking about quantum mechanics, one can steer clear of philosophical difficulties as long as one confines oneself to what is measured. Things get very confusing philosophically, however, if one starts to worry about what the world is like between measurements and about how physical reality is in itself and not just how it presents itself to us in the results of our measurements. An easy way out, therefore, is to say that physics is just about phenomena, appearances, and measurements, and many physicists took this way out, at least rhetorically.

These symptoms of positivist thinking among physicists were deceptive. Though Einstein was originally influenced by Mach, the theory of gravity he ended up with is actually not Machian in character. When Heisenberg urged upon Einstein positivist ideas as the right way to think about quantum mechanics, on the grounds that Einstein himself had reasoned in this way when developing relativity, Einstein retorted, "Possibly I did use this kind of reasoning, but it is nonsense all the same."[18] Einstein, as it turned out, was very much a philosophical realist. And because he couldn't see how to understand quantum mechanics in a realist way, he notoriously rejected it as an incomplete theory.

The truth is that scientists are overwhelmingly philosophical realists. They believe that science tells one about reality and not merely about appearances or the readings on the dials of one's experimental devices. That is why they are as philosophically puzzled about quantum mechanics as everyone else. (Though it should be noted, there are realist ways of understanding quantum mechanics.)

18. Heisenberg, *Physics and Beyond*, 63.

Allow me to quote Dougherty again: "The British empiricists, as well as Comte [the father of positivism], failed to pay much attention to the actual practice in the sciences of their day, practices that in no way and in none of its parts were in accord with their positivist schemes."[19] Paradoxically enough, though, as I noted before, a very strong influence of positivism can be seen in much Catholic writing about modern science. How did this come about? It came about largely through the influence of Pierre Duhem and Jacques Maritain. Duhem, who lived from 1861 to 1916, was a distinguished scientist and an important historian and philosopher of science. As a philosopher of science, he was a thoroughgoing and avowed positivist, but a positivist of an unusual kind.

A main principle of the positivists was the rejection of metaphysics, which for them included the notion that there is a reality underlying appearances and phenomena. Duhem agreed with other positivists in saying that modern science was only about appearances and phenomena and had nothing to say about underlying reality. Unlike them, however, Duhem believed in such a reality, but maintained that only Aristotelian-Thomistic metaphysics could give one access to it. So there were two kinds of knowledge in his scheme: the knowledge of appearances given by modern science, and the knowledge of being given by Aristotelian-Thomistic metaphysics.

Jacques Maritain had very similar ideas, and through him, they profoundly shaped much neo-Thomist thinking about science. Here is how Michal Heller, the Polish priest, physicist and philosopher describes the situation:

> The neo-thomistic approach to the sciences . . . had two roots. The first root . . . went back to Aristotle and St. Thomas Aquinas. . . . Maritain and others applied [Aristotle's] theory of knowledge to the modern sciences and supplemented it with suitably modified elements of the [then] current philosophy of science. This was the second root. . . . However, the [then] current philosophy of science was mainly of . . . [positivistic] origin. [It] assumed that [as] no essences exist, one can meaningfully speak only about appearances. Neo-thomists took over his doctrine, but modified it by claiming that whereas science investigates phenomena, philosophy penetrates into the essences of things.[20]

19. Dougherty, *Nature of Scientific Explanation*, 9.
20. Heller, *Creative Tension*, 72.

William A. Wallace, one of the leaders of the River Forest school of Thomism, gives a similar account.[21]

The positivism that infiltrated Catholic thinking and discourse about science in this way has interfered with genuine theological engagement with modern science. It has also sometimes led Catholic authors to make bizarre statements, of which I would rather not give instances.

It is easy to understand the appeal of these ideas. They allow one to put modern science in a box. If it doesn't tell you about reality, then it cannot do any harm philosophically. And in particular it cannot do harm to religion.

Finally, there is the criticism that the focus of modern science on the quantitative and measurable leads it astray philosophically. This is a complicated topic. So, rather than attempt to discuss it here, I refer the reader to a talk I gave in the summer of 2016, which is published in the American Catholic Philosophical Quarterly.[22] Here I will only say that for a variety of reasons some Catholic thinkers have failed properly to understand the mathematization of modern physical science and how deeply it allows us to grasp the natures, essences and causes of things—at least inanimate things.

A HOPEFUL FUTURE

Up to now, most of this article has been somewhat negative in tone, but my main message is actually hopeful. What I have been negative about are the negative views of modern science one finds in some Catholic discourse about it. I have been so, because I think modern science is our friend if we look at it in the right light, and if we think long-term. If we really believe that the truths of science and the truths of faith cannot contradict each other, then we ought to have confidence that as science progresses apparent difficulties will be resolved and that seeming dangers will prove illusory. We should expect scientific breakthroughs to narrow the distance between scientific perspectives and religious ones, not to increase them. I will now briefly discuss five major developments in twentieth-century physics that bear out this expectation. Those interested in a more extended discussion of them are invited to consult my book *Modern Physics and Ancient Faith*.

The first development is the discovery of the Big Bang. For a long while, it seemed that modern science was pointing to a universe that had no temporal beginning. The idea of a "Beginning" came increasingly to be

21. Wallace, *Modeling of Nature*, 224–28.

22. Barr, "Mathematization of Physics."

seen as a relic of outmoded religious mythology. The discovery in physics that "energy can neither be created nor destroyed," the discovery that the number of atoms does not change in chemical reactions, and the fact that it seemed unnatural for space and time coordinates to be bounded, all suggested a universe that is unbounded in time. Einstein's theory of General Relativity and the Big Bang theory that was based upon it showed that it was possible and even probable that the universe—and time itself—had a beginning. Evidence for the Big Bang is now overwhelming. It is possible that the Big Bang was not the beginning of the universe and that something preceded it. Nevertheless, there are strong theoretical reasons to think that the universe had a temporal beginning, if not at the Big Bang then earlier.

I am not that sympathetic to attempts to prove the existence of God from the finite age of the universe, and in particular to the so-called Kalam Argument. I think that temporal beginning and creation are distinct ideas, as St. Thomas Aquinas himself understood. Nevertheless, the discovery of the Big Bang certainly brings the scientific picture of the world closer to the religious view and further from the view clearly preferred by many atheists.

The second development has been the discovery that the laws of physics form a beautiful, harmonious, intricate and unified mathematical structure based on very profound ideas. The mathematization of physics, which has been looked at askance by some Catholic thinkers, as I have noted, has in fact revealed this wonderful truth to us. Hermann Weyl, one of the great mathematicians and mathematical physicists of the twentieth century gave a lecture in 1931, in which he said, "Many people think that modern science is far removed from God. I find, on the contrary . . . that in our knowledge of physical nature, we have penetrated so far that we can obtain a vision of the flawless harmony that is in conformity with sublime reason."[23]

We have since then penetrated the mathematical secrets of nature much further. One of the most brilliant physicists in the world, Edward Witten, who describes himself as a skeptical agnostic, said the following in an interview several years ago:

> The laws of nature as they've been uncovered in the last few centuries, and especially . . . in the last century, are very surprising. They are very subtle. . . . They've got a great beauty, which is a little hard to describe, maybe, if one hasn't experienced it. . . . The laws as we know them are very beautiful mathematically. They involve

23. Weyl, *Open World*, 54–55.

very interesting and subtle concepts. . . . It is a rich story, and it all hangs together beautifully.[24]

In a much earlier interview, Witten was equally rhapsodic about so-called superstring theory, which he and many other top theoretical physicists regard as the most probable candidate for the ultimate theory of physics. He said to the interviewer, "I don't think I've succeeded in conveying to you its wonder, incredible consistency, remarkable elegance, and beauty."[25]

The third development, which has unfolded mostly over the last forty years, and especially the last twenty, has been the realization that the laws of physics have many features that are just right to make the existence of life possible. These are sometimes called "anthropic coincidences." Some of these concern parameters that appear in the laws of physics having numerical values that seem "fine-tuned" to make life possible. This has opened people's eyes, including the eyes of some scientists and philosophers, to the possibility of purpose in nature. I will quote Ed Witten again. He may not see in these coincidences evidence of purpose, but he is obviously deeply impressed by them. He said,

> The laws of nature are very delicate. . . . Just with physics we already know, [the fact] that galaxies, stars and planets roughly like ours could have formed, and that living things roughly like us could have formed, depends on many details of the laws of physics as we currently know them being just the way they are and not being slightly different. [I think] we'll never resolve the sense of wonder about that.[26]

The fourth development is the overthrow of determinism by quantum mechanics in the 1920s and 1930s. As I mentioned, the determinism of Newtonian physics and classical physics as a whole created serious difficulties for belief in human free will—or at least for the possibility that a freely acting person could affect the physical world by his decisions. It led to the concept, still taken as dogma by most materialists, that the physical world is "causally closed." So the overthrow of determinism was an enormous positive development from the viewpoint of traditional theism.

24. "Of Beauty and Consolation."
25. Witten quoted in Horgan, *End of Science*.
26. "Of Beauty and Consolation."

The fifth positive development is that a powerful anti-materialist argument emerges from the basic characteristics of quantum mechanics. What has vexed so many philosophers and physicists about quantum mechanics concerns what is called "the measurement problem." The attempts to grapple with this have led many people in strange philosophical directions. A strong argument can be made, however, that the measurement problem arises only if one accepts materialism or physicalism as a premise. In the words of the distinguished philosopher of physics Hans Halvorson of Princeton University, "In the case of quantum mechanics, if one presupposes physicalism, then one quickly lands in the measurement problem."[27] That is why several eminent physicists of the twentieth century, such as Eugene Wigner and Sir Rudolf Peierls, argued on the basis of quantum mechanics that materialism is false and that the mind or consciousness is not reducible to physics.

The traditional interpretation of quantum mechanics thus has *two* profound implications favorable to the Catholic conception of the world: it undermines both determinism and physicalism. It is ironic, therefore, that many Catholic thinkers—for example, Stanley Jaki, Mortimer Adler, and the physicist Peter E. Hodgson—have regarded the traditional interpretation of quantum mechanics as posing a philosophical and theological danger. Their worry was that it could not be reconciled with a realist view of science. They were in good company, because Einstein had the same concern, as I have mentioned. As Hans Halvorson noted, though, some of the philosophical conundrums of quantum mechanics arise only if one adopts physicalist premises. And since many philosophers and physicists do adopt those premises, quantum mechanics has seemed more dangerous to a sound and traditional metaphysics than it really is. This is a case where modern physics is much more of a friend to traditional religious belief than many Catholic thinkers have understood.

The five developments I just briefly surveyed are all taken from physics, yet there are equally important developments that one can point to in other fields. For example, in the early days of evolutionary theory, it was not clear on whether human beings had emerged in one location or by parallel development in many widely separated locations, as postulated by so-called "multiregional theories" of human origins. Each view had its defenders. The multiregional view would obviously be quite problematic for Catholic

27. Halvorson, "Quantum Mechanics and the Soul," 163.

theology, as it would imperil the original unity of the human race, with implications for Original Sin and other doctrines. This was something that naturally concerned the magisterium. In recent decades, however, evidence has come strongly to favor the idea that *Homo sapiens* emerged in one location, in a geographically very small area, with an original population that numbered in the few thousands.[28]

Just as remarkable are recent ideas on the origins of human language. In a new book that may well prove to be epoch-making, Robert Berwick and Noam Chomsky make the case very powerfully for what might be called a Big Bang theory of the emergence of human language. Using a variety of very sophisticated arguments and discoveries in linguistics, computer science, neuroscience, evolutionary theory, the study of animal communication, and other fields, they argue (a) that no other animals have language—even in rudimentary form—in the sense that humans do (i.e., recursively infinite syntactical language, as needed for abstract thought), (b) that human language was first an instrument of thought rather than communication, and (c) that this capacity emerged very suddenly, probably over a single generation, and likely in a single individual, as a result of a small number of fortuitous mutations. Just as interestingly, they make the following statement:

> The atomic elements [of human language] pose deep mysteries. The minimal meaning-bearing elements of human languages— word-like but not words—are radically different from anything known in animal communication systems. Their origin is entirely obscure, posing a very serious problem for the evolution of human cognitive capacities, language in particular. . . . The problem is severe, and is insufficiently recognized and understood."[29]

What they are saying is that while one can explain in evolutionary terms how the capacity arose to manipulate word-like, meaning-bearing units, it is mysterious how the first such units themselves arose. To put it simply, concepts to manipulate and the ability to manipulate concepts have to appear together, and that is very hard to explain.

---

28. The development of *Homo sapiens* after the species emerged in Africa has involved a small amount of multiregional influence: there were interbreeding events with "archaic" species of *Homo* that had emerged in Eurasia, including Neanderthals and Denisovans, leaving an imprint on the human genome.

29. Berwick and Chomsky, *Why Only Us*, 90.

Finally, I would note that it is becoming more common for philosophers and scientists to admit that consciousness cannot be explained in physicalist terms. The philosopher David Chalmers created a sensation back in 1997 with his book *The Conscious Mind: In Search of a Fundamental Theory*, in which he made this case. The eminent philosopher Thomas Nagel scandalized his fellow atheists when he argued the same point (among others) very forcefully in his 2012 book *Mind and Cosmos*. It has become respectable for philosophers to refer to the "hard problem of consciousness," a term coined by Chalmers. I would state the problem this way: given a complete description of any physical system as that would be understood by modern physics, there is no way in principle to deduce from it, mathematically or logically, any conclusion about whether that system is conscious and has subjective experiences. I think this follows obviously from the nature of modern physics. Here is what Ed Witten, in the same interview I quoted twice before, said about this:

> I tend to think consciousness will be a mystery. That's what I tend to believe. I tend to think that the workings of the conscious brain will be elucidated to a large extent [and] . . . that biologists, with perhaps physicists contributing, will understand much better how the brain works. But why something that we call consciousness goes with those workings I think will remain mysterious. Perhaps I'm mistaken. I have a much easier time imagining how we'd understand the Big Bang, even though we can't do it yet, than I can imagine understanding consciousness. . . . I am not going to attempt to define consciousness. In a way that is connected to fact that I don't think it will become part of physics. . . . I am skeptical that it's going to become part of physics.[30]

Saying it will not become a part of physics, is tantamount to saying that physicalism cannot account for it.

To conclude, I think that time is on the side of religious belief as far as the actual discoveries of science are concerned. In the long run, science converges on the truth concerning the things it can study, and—to the extent that it does so—it must in the long run be the friend of revealed truth. To the extent that scientific discoveries or theories sometimes seem inimical or dangerous to theology or sound philosophy, it is not because modern science is defective in its methods, but because modern science is still incomplete. It is still *in via*, still on the road. Nevertheless, whatever the

30. "Of Beauty and Consolation."

twists and turns in that road, whatever labyrinthine ways science follows in pursuing its goals—we should be confident about where it must ultimately lead.[31]

---

31. A note from the editors: We are grateful to Jay Martin for his invaluable assistance in editing this essay, in addition to discussing this book project more broadly with us, from conception to completion. Along with three of his colleagues, including John Cavadini, Jay recently received the annual "Expanded Reason Award" from the Ratzinger Foundation at the University of Madrid for his work on the Science and Religion initiative through the McGrath Institute for Church Life. This international recognition testifies to the visionary energy and practical follow through of the McGrath Institute for Church Life, under Cavadini's direction, for the renewed pedagogy concerning the relationship of science and religion in the modern world, much in keeping with the aims of the present essay. For more on the award, please visit expandedreasonawards.org.

9

What We Hold in Trust

Melanie M. Morey

On April 16, 2009, Dr. John Cavadini welcomed participants to the opening day of a new initiative offered by the University of Notre Dame's McGrath Institute for Church Life. *What We Hold in Trust: A Seminar for Catholic College and University Trustees* was convened to address a critical issue facing Catholic higher education: how to prepare and form Catholic collegiate and university trustees effectively to execute fiduciary responsibility at the institutions they serve.

The seminar Cavadini designed was remarkable in a number of ways. It was the first formal gathering on governance hosted by a Catholic institution for Catholic college and university trustees and presidents. It was also remarkable for requiring each participating institution to send a governance team that included the president, the board chair, and one other trustee. And finally, because "there is no single way for a Catholic college or university to understand and actualize its Catholic mission,"[1] Cavadini insisted that participants represent the full range of Catholic institutions in the United States. He believed that trustees and presidents from very different types of institutions would benefit from spending time together addressing the critical issue of governance. The experience of seminar participants proved he was correct.[2]

1. Morey and Piderit, *Catholic Higher Education*, 21.
2. The following institutions participated in "What We Hold in Trust" seminars:

College and university trustees have and must exercise fiduciary responsibility, regardless of the institutions in which they serve. Rooted in the Latin term *fiduciaries,* this responsibility means to hold in trust or in faith. But what exactly is it that collegiate and university trustees hold in trust?

The Association of Governing Boards addressed this question in the March/April 2013 issue of their magazine *Trusteeship* in a wide-ranging interview with a half dozen experts in the area of collegiate and university governance. A major takeaway from the interview was that,

> It is not enough (for trustees) to protect the institution's endowment. Trustees must look to the future and execute their duties with loyalty, faith, and trust. . . . They must ensure fidelity to mission, integrity of operations, and conservation of core values; and they must safeguard the institution's moral compass.[3]

CONTEXT

These are challenging decades for Catholic college and university trustees and much is being asked of them as they help navigate the way forward for their institutions. Catholic colleges and universities struggle to survive in the American market place as thriving and reputable institutions of higher learning that are truly and faithfully Catholic. This struggle is not a new struggle, a fact documented by a great body of literature.[4] What is new is that over the course of the last fifty years concerns about Catholic colleges

---

Alvernia University, Reading, PA; Assumption College, Worcester, MA; Cabrini University, Radnor, PA; Canisius College, Buffalo, NY; Clarke University, Dubuque, IA; Franciscan University of Steubenville, Steubenville, OH; Holy Cross Collee, Notre Dame, IN; John Carroll University, University Heights, OH; King's College, Wilkes-Barre, PA; Loras College, Dubuque, IA; Manhattan College, Riverdale, NY; Marian University, Indianapolis, IN; Mount St. Mary's University, Emmitsburg, MD; Saint Anselm College, Manchester, NH; Siena College, Loudonville, NY; St. Bonaventure University, St. Bonaventure, NY; St. Joseph University, Philadelphia, PA; St. Mary's University of Minnesota, Winona, MN; University of Portland, Portland, OR; University of St. Francis, Fort Wayne, IN; and Villanova University, Villanova, PA

3. "Fiduciary Behavior."

4. See Burtchaell, *Dying of the Light*; Gallin, *Negotiating Identity*; Gleason, *Contending with Modernity*; Hesburgh, *Challenge and Promise of a Catholic University*; O'Brien, *Idea of a Catholic University*; Morey and Piderit, *Catholic Higher Education*; Dosen, *Catholic Higher Education in the 1960s*; and Smith and Cavadini, *Building Catholic Higher Education*, to name a few.

and universities have shifted from primarily doubts about their academic quality to questions about their Catholicity.

For much of their early history Catholic colleges and universities were seen often as second-rate and narrowly parochial institutions. In 1955 that began to change when Msgr. John Tracy Ellis set off paroxysms of concern and recrimination among those inside Catholic higher education with his essay "American Catholics and the Intellectual Life." In the essay Ellis not only charged Catholic colleges and universities specifically with having low academic standards and failing to stress intellectual excellence, he also challenged American Catholics' commitment to the intellectual life in general.[5] This criticism resonated with those in the Catholic academy and prompted a reform movement "structured by the academy's definition of academic excellence centered on academic freedom and enhanced by institutional autonomy."[6]

Prior to the 1960s, questions about institutional Catholic identity in colleges and universities never came up. Everyone knew these institutions were Catholic. Almost all were owned, operated, and governed by the religious institutes that founded them. Some of them had lay trustees, but these lay trustees served purely in an advisory capacity to the leadership of the religious institutes.[7]

Beginning around 1964 colleges began to include more and more lay people on boards. The historian, Philip Gleason, lists four major factors that contributed to this rapid turn toward laicization. First, leaders were responding to the teachings of Vatican II on the role of lay people in the Church. Second, presidents realized they needed more expertise, especially in financial matters, than was available within their own religious orders. Third, future streams of government dollars were being threatened at the time because of a legal ruling in the *Horace Mann* case. And finally, the "McGrath thesis" helped to quell internal resistance from nuns and brothers and priests opposed to relinquishing congregational authority over the schools.[8]

---

5. Ellis, "American Catholics."

6. Morey, "Way We Were," 279.

7. Gallin, *Independence*, xi.

8. The McGrath thesis was named after Reverend John J. McGrath, who wrote a monograph arguing that because these institutions were formed for charitable purposes, they did not belong to the religious institutes; rather, they belonged to the general public whom they served. See Gleason, *Contending with Modernity*, 317–18.

There is no question that in the 1960s Catholic higher education leaders pursued laicization as a positive step forward for their institutions. What they neither desired nor intended, however, was secularization. But, as Alice Gallin, OSU, points out, their efforts had unintended consequences that helped pave the way for it to take hold.

> In 1960 there was still a great predominance of members of the founding religious community at every level of Catholic institutions. By 1990 they constituted a small minority. . . . [Laicization] was a movement that impacted on the ever-present question of Catholic identity. For while 'laicization' should never be confused with 'secularization' (used pejoratively), the predominance of lay men and women in the college's internal constituency meant that the relationship of the college to the church no longer had a clear canonical character as an apostolic work of a religious community.[9]

Laicization of boards was one element of a much larger reframing of the relationship between the Catholic academy and ecclesial authority. A more dramatic element came with the release of the Land O'Lakes Statement in 1967. In its openings paragraphs, its twenty-six signatories declared that in order,

> to perform its teaching and research functions effectively the Catholic university must have a true autonomy and academic freedom in the face of authority of whatever kind, lay or clerical, external to the academic community itself. To say this is simply to assert that institutional autonomy and academic freedom are essential conditions of life and growth and indeed of survival for Catholic universities as for all universities.[10]

Land O' Lakes represented a pivotal moment in Catholic higher education that for some came to represent not only change, but also betrayal—a view that in some circles intensified over time. One of the most strident among the latter day critics, Fr. George Rutler, marked the fiftieth anniversary of the statement by insisting "the Land O'Lakes Conference was to higher Catholic education what the Yalta Conference was to Eastern Europe."[11] Notre Dame's president, Fr. John Jenkins, CSC, on the other hand, praised the statement's confident vision of the Catholic university, seldom

9. Gallin, *Negotiating Identity*, 113–14.

10. Gallin, *American Catholic Higher Education*, 7–12.

11. Rutler, "Idea of a Catholic University."

referenced by lamenters, as "a community of learners or . . . scholars, in which Catholicism is perceptibly present and effectively operative."[12]

The Land O'Lakes Statement helped change dispositions and sparked a vigorous conversation about what a Catholic university could, should, and would be in the modern context. In the following years a number of other documents helped move the discussion along.[13] Finally, in 1990, Pope John Paul II's apostolic constitution *Ex corde ecclesiae* opened a dramatic new chapter in the discussion.

Although the first part of the constitution took a decidedly pastoral tone and was generally well received, its accompanying call for juridical norms for implementation struck a discordant note among almost all in the American Catholic academy. What resulted was a torrent of rancorous debate about what constitutes the appropriate limits of ecclesial authority and control over Catholic higher education that went on for well over a decade. Because the discussion was so bold and loud, it consumed everyone's attention and sidelined other pressing issues. Consequently, as the intensifying forces of secularism buffeted Catholic colleges and universities, no one was asking how best to cultivate the unique Catholic culture and character of colleges and universities in an increasingly challenging environment.

It was during this stormy fifty-year period that lay trustees were assuming ultimate responsibility for the future of Catholic higher education. These generous and committed individuals took up their responsibilities with enthusiasm. But far too often they did so with a major information deficit regarding what constitutes collegiate Catholic identity and their particular responsibilities in light of it. And they did so at a time when the members of sponsoring religious institutes on whom so many lay trustees relied in "all things Catholic" began playing a much diminished role. Furthermore, lay trustees were frequently alumni or alumnae of the very institution they were asked to serve. Their knowledge of the Catholicity of the institution was heavily influenced by their own experience as students. While trustees realized things had changed and there were far fewer nuns, brothers, or priests, they assumed that the new lay faculty were similarly competent and committed to the faith. In fact, many, if not most, had neither the preparation to integrate the Catholic intellectual tradition, nor the

---

12. Jenkins, "Land O'Lakes."

13. Delegates of the Second Congress of Catholic Universities, "Catholic University in the Modern World"; John Paul II, *Sapientia Christiana*; *Code of Canon Law*.

inclination to do so. Their primary goals and practices were all too similar to those of faculty and administrators in non-religious institutions.

It is true that sponsoring religious institutes established mission departments and hired mission officers. They also developed elaborate training programs for trustees. But in almost all cases these mission efforts focused more on the charism of the religious institute than on what constitutes the essential Catholic character of colleges and universities.

A NEW APPROACH TO FORMATION

The *What We Hold in Trust Seminar* was structured to address what had been missing in trustee formation programs designed during an almost fifty-year period of rapid change in Catholic higher education. It identified three things that affect trustees' capacity to execute their fiduciary responsibility: a particular operational conviction, personal qualifications demanded by the governance role, and a robust understanding of what constitutes the unique nature of Catholic colleges and universities. The seminar also offered an array of common sense practices for enhancing trustee performance.

Operational Conviction and Personal Qualifications

During his session titled, "Faculty and Administrators in the Age of the Laity," the late Rev. Richard P. McBrien forthrightly addressed both a necessary operational conviction for trustees and the personal capacities they should bring to their work and cultivate. According to McBrien, far too often Catholic college and university trustees, as well as administrators and faculty, operate with a minimalist criterion regarding Catholic identity. It is one that asks, "What is the least that we can settle for and still be a Catholic institution?" This approach is not just insufficient to assure the vitality of mission, core values, and the institution's moral compass, it actually undermines them. To McBrien's mind, something far bolder and more expansive is essential if these institutions are going to survive and thrive. Trustees, McBrien insisted, must always "operate on the assumption—and the conviction—that it is possible to be *both* a first-rate academic institution *and* one that is truly Catholic."

McBrien enthusiastically applauded the growing laicization of governance and leadership in Catholic higher education as the work of the Holy

Spirit. He insisted, however, that those lay people have the capacity to do the task they have accepted. Capacity equal to the high responsibility of insuring and enhancing the unique character and mission of Catholic colleges and universities, according to McBrien, is more than a benign disposition toward the tradition. Individuals chosen to be trustees and administrators "must have demonstrated experience in Catholic higher education and be cognizant of major issues and developments in the Catholic Church."[14] Trustees and administrators do not need to be theologians, to be sure. But a critical mass of them should have an adult understanding of Catholic theology, Catholic culture, and the Catholic intellectual tradition. In choosing those who might join their ranks, trustees should have a keen eye for and commitment to this level of Catholic competence. Otherwise boards will not be able to execute their duties responsibly.

The Character of a Catholic University

In his opening remarks at the convening of the first *What We Hold in Trust Seminar*, John Cavadini shared with trustees a way to better understand the unique character of a Catholic college or university. He proposed that they think of the university as both a place of witness *and* a place dialogue. The absence of either, he suggested, would be crippling in terms of meeting the full purpose of a university. If it were only a place of witness, with no room for dialogue, the university would not be a credible place of higher learning. Equally, if it were only a place of dialogue, with no ultimate values worth bearing witness to, there would be little purpose for dialogue.[15]

Catholic colleges and universities, if they are to be faithful to their mission as both Catholic and institutions of higher learning, must be places of witness, rooted in the evangelizing mission of the Church, and places of dialogue where real thinking is possible, according to Cavadini. Neither alone can assure the integrity of Catholic high education. The responsibility to assure they are both belongs to trustees but it is not an easy thing to assure. In fact, it can be a real struggle. On one side Catholic colleges and universities are pulled by the forces of secularism which dilute Catholic witness. On the other side, they are pulled by the forces of sectarianism, which Christian Smith tells us can, "easily lead to an insular, defensive

14. McBrien, "Students, Faculty, and Administrators."

15. Cavadini, "Introductory Comments."

posture that does not embody the best of the Catholic tradition."[16] Trustees of Catholic colleges and universities must help their institutions resist the pull of these forces of imbalance.

The witness of a Catholic college or university, Cavadini clarified, is connected to the evangelizing mission of the Church. But, because the university is not the same as the Church and because it is a place of dialogue as well as witness, the witness must be situated in "the very thing that makes a university a university—namely, its intellectual life."[17] Critical and unique to that intellectual life at a Catholic college or university is the presence of a Theology Department. "Having theology represented as an academic discipline in a college or university," Cavadini points out, "implies the academic community shares an openness to the idea of an integration of knowledge. It means the institution has the possibility of succeeding in its academic endeavor because, in order to be truly integrative and not simply interdisciplinary, the conversation at some point necessarily becomes theological." Theology, the study of God, is, as St. Anselm famously put it, "faith seeking understanding."[18]

As critical as theology departments are to Catholic colleges and universities, witness is not confined to them alone. Rather, the entire culture at these Catholic institutions gives witness to "faith seeking understanding." "This Catholic approach," Cavadini makes clear, "generates a kind of thick intellectual culture, shot through at once with mystery and reason. Irreducible mystery is always in the lead, shining beneath and giving the culture its shape, even as that culture takes on life in its puzzling over the results of all other disciplinary research."[19]

PERFORMANCE

There is little agreement among governing boards about performance metrics for higher education.[20] That is even truer at Catholic colleges and universities, particularly in the critical areas of Catholic institutional identity and culture. The former president of Princeton University, William Bowen, provides a colorful description of the situation: "[Governing boards] are

16. Smith and Cavadini, *Building Catholic Higher Education*, ix.
17. Cavadini, "Introductory Comments."
18. Cavadini, "Theology at a Catholic University."
19. Cavadini, "Theology at a Catholic University."
20. Chait et al., *Improving the Performance of Governing Boards*, 14.

notoriously subject to the problem of failing to see a fast, clearly visible train coming—even when it is moving inexorably and their organization is sitting right on the tracks."[21] If higher education boards are to have any hope of becoming more adept at avoiding collisions, they must get better at performing their oversight role. Adopting or changing some of their usual practices can help them be better practitioners. The presenters at the *What We Hold in Trust Seminars* offered a number of important suggestions for improving performance.

Saint Anselm College president, Fr. Jonathan DeFelice, OSB, urged trustees to attend carefully to institutional mission statements, underscoring that they must ensure that the statements "clearly express" the college's or university's Catholic nature.[22] For one thing, publicly claiming Catholic identity is a matter of institutional integrity. It also is the first necessary step toward establishing effective policies and practices that implement Catholic institutional character, culture, and mission. Failure to clarify Catholic character and mission implies a willingness by trustees to "hedge their bets" in the higher education marketplace which puts a Catholic college or university at risk for increased secularization.

Sr. Marylouise Fennel, RSM, reminded the trustees their most important obligation is choosing a president and their second obligation is supporting that president.[23] At a Catholic college or university, choosing a president requires attention to Catholic leadership capacity. Fennell makes clear that being a practicing Catholic is not a sufficient qualification for a presidential candidate in a Catholic institution. Nor is personal faith and acceptance of Church teachings enough. She agrees with McBrien that much more must be expected of would-be presidents. Candidates should have some personal experience in a Catholic college or university. They should also have a sophisticated understanding of Catholic theology and awareness of current and recent developments in the Catholic Church.

Once chosen, a president needs the ongoing support of the governing board. In matters pertaining to Catholic culture and character trustees should signal a direction in which they want the president to move and then be clear they are with the president. If the direction is a change or adjustment, trustee support is all the more important. A clear and unambiguous statement by the board "sends a strong signal to the whole community

21. Bowen, *Inside the Boardroom*, 24.
22. DeFelice, "Faith and Academic Life."
23. Fennell, "Faith and Law."

about the importance of Catholic identity and further strengthens the hand of the president in efforts to realize goals."[24]

In order to fulfill their responsibilities, trustees need succinct, forthright, and strategic information about institutional Catholic culture at their institution.[25] Rev. William J. Byron, SJ, specified what kind of information, beyond the annual financial audit, a board needs to work effectively:

> Trustees should see an annual report from all units of the institution describing in both quantitative and qualitative terms the extent of each unit's contribution to the advancement of the Catholic character of the institution, as expressed in the institution's published mission statement. If that statement is insufficiently precise to enable such reporting, trustees should instruct management to produce an annual report form with reporting categories that describe measurable aspects of Catholic identity.[26]

Another critical issue trustees must address is how to assure that Catholic colleges and universities have the human capital necessary to strengthen Catholic culture, character, and mission and academic excellence. Dr. John Affleck-Graves, the Executive Vice-President at Notre Dame, pointed out two significant steps trustees at the University of Notre Dame have taken to meet this challenge. First, the trustees define in percentage terms what constitutes the critical mass of Catholic faculty and students necessary to ensure fidelity to institutional mission. This is necessary, but not sufficient. Not all Catholic faculty are either interested in or committed to furthering the Catholic identity of the institution. And not all Catholic students and faculty practice the faith. Therefore, institutions must find ways to actively pursue the best candidates. Otherwise they will not be able to address the critical issue of human capital. One governing board that has done a lot is Notre Dame's.

In 2006 Notre Dame's president, Fr. Jenkins, announced that Rev. Robert Sullivan was being put in charge of an effort to identify able Catholic scholars. He also was being asked to sit on an ad hoc committee focused on recruiting outstanding Catholic faculty members. "There often appears to be a disconnect," Sullivan said, "between a seemingly abstract commitment to recruit 'Catholic intellectuals' and the nuts and bolts, give-and-take of hiring on the ground." The effort he heads at Notre Dame is designed to

24. Morey and Piderit, *Catholic Higher Education*, 293.
25. Morey and Piderit, *Catholic Higher Education*, 295.
26. Byron, "Catholic Higher Education."

establish a "search engine to systematically identify and recruit such intellectuals in considerable numbers."[27]

Not all schools can adopt the Notre Dame approach, to be sure. Notre Dame has a rare advantage of being both financially well-positioned and outstanding academically. But regardless of their academic reputation and financial where-with-all, every Catholic college or university must address this particular capacity issue. At the barest minimum all institutions should adopt a policy of preferential hiring of Catholics. It is a sensible approach that trustees can rather easily endorse. "Catholic institutions have the right to preferentially hire Catholics," according to Affleck-Graves, "because it is a *bona fide* occupational qualification."[28]

In order to ensure that their institutions have the necessary human capital, Catholic colleges and universities have two choices. Hire people who already are well prepared or develop a way to form those who are not prepared that they hire. A place like the University of Notre Dame is in a good place to hire such talent—and they are having trouble doing it. It is far more difficult for most other Catholic colleges and universities.

For a good long time religious institutes of men and women formed and educated their own members who then served in the colleges and universities. Given the contraction in religious congregations and the change in ministerial focus among them, it is no longer reasonable to think they can do much to help assure a critical mass of talent. And presently there is no formal formation farm system that serves Catholic higher education. The current situation is critical and demands a bold response. Catholic college and university trustees will have to be part of developing that response.

CONCLUSION

Fifty years ago laicization of Catholic college and university governance began in earnest. This welcome development has grown stronger over time, not only in colleges and universities but in all types of Catholic institutions. There is no question that the American Church has benefitted by the generous gifts of time, treasure, and talent lay trustees have contributed over the years. And the Church will continue to rely on them in the future. But while the Church has accepted this generosity, she has not matched it with

27. Conklin, "How Catholic the Faculty?"
28. Affleck-Graves, "Catholic Mission."

the critically important formation and education trustees need to exercise faithfully their unique fiduciary responsibilities.

The *What We Hold in Trust Seminars* provided a great service for college and university presidents and trustees and for the Church. They were structured in a unique way to meet a pressing need in Catholic higher education—and did so admirably. But the need still exists and it goes well beyond colleges and universities. It exists among the full range of Catholic institutions that rely on lay governance to assure that they demonstrate excellence in their fields and maintain a vibrant Catholic character and identity. The McGrath Institute for Church Life provided timely leadership when it instituted the *What We Hold in Trust Seminars*—and set a high bar doing so.

Now it is time to build on what John Cavadini started.

PART 3

Ecclesial Vision:
The Church in the Modern World

10

The Ecclesial Nature of Theology and the Unity of *Doctrina* and *Vita*

Michael Heintz

It is fair to say that John Cavadini has a deep affection and respect for Origen, the third-century theologian. This is not because Cavadini is given to identifying himself with the theologically edgy, much less because of Origen's admittedly more speculative views which never became part of the larger Tradition. Rather, it is because Origen was, and always considered himself to be, a man of the Church. Origen's remark, in his *Homilies on Luke*,[1] that he desired to be a "man of the Church," is precisely why John has been so attentive to Origen as a reader of Scripture, a theologian, and an *ecclesiasticus*.[2]

---

1. *Ego vero, qui opto esse ecclesiasticus et non ab haeresiarchae aliquo, sed a Christo vocabulo nuncupari et habere nomen, quod benedicitur super terram, et cupio tam opere quam sensu et esse et dici christianus*: "But I, who wish to be a man of the Church and to take the name not of some heretic, but of Christ, and to hold fast to that name which is blessed upon earth, desire both in deed and in mind to be and to be called a Christian" (Origen, "Homily 16.6," 87:244). Hans Urs von Balthasar had chosen these words as the inscription to his anthology of Origen's writings in Balthasar, *Spirit and Fire* (cf. de Lubac, *History and Spirit*, 60–63).

2. As witness of this, one should consult John Cavadini's beautiful and profound essay, a thought-provoking meditation on the Church in light of Origen's engagement with the Scriptures. See Cavadini, "Church as the Sacrament of Creation."

Cavadini's work as theologian, as professor to both undergraduates and graduate students, as director of the McGrath Institute for Church Life, as colleague to those of us blessed by his friendship and example, as mentor for younger theologians, as consultant to his own bishop and other bishops (including the Bishop of Rome), bespeak his commitment to theology as an ecclesial discipline. One expression of this commitment has been the formation of seminarians for priesthood and of young men and women for lay ecclesial ministry through the Master of Divinity Program in the Theology Department at the University of Notre Dame. In his teaching and formation work (including a very popular course on the priesthood, taught to seminarians for the Congregation of Holy Cross), Cavadini witnesses to and communicates a deep love for the Church, its living Tradition, and the life which it embodies.

Near the beginning of his massive *Commentary on John*, Origen remarks, almost in passing and no doubt with reference to the Evangelist himself, that if one wishes to understand the Gospel, he must first learn to recline on the breast of the Lord and to receive from the Lord Mary as his mother.[3] Jesus, the one "sent" from the Father, the Word now made flesh, who dwells eternally εἰς τὸν κόλπον τοῦ πατρός (John 1:18),[4] continues his mission in time and space through those who likewise have been "sent" (John 20:21); however, those sent must first learn to recline ἐν τῷ κόλπῳ τοῦ Ἰησοῦ (John 13:23). And just as the Only-begotten, who dwells *in sinum Patris*, has "exegeted" (ἐξηγήσατο, 1:18) the Father, making him known, so too only those who come to share such intimacy with the Word-made-flesh and who have been entrusted by him to his Mother, can come to understand the Gospel and communicate it to others.

---

3. Origen, *Commentary on John*, 1.4(6). Commentary on John 1.4(6): τολμητέον τοί νυν εἰπεῖν ἀπαρχὴν μὲν πασῶν γραφῶν εἶναι τὰεὐαγγέλια, τῶν δὲ εὐαγγελίων ἀπαρχὴν τὸ κατὰ Ἰωάννην, οὗ τὸν νοῦν οὐδεὶς δύναται λαβεῖνμὴ ἀναπεσὼν ἐπὶ τὸ στῆθος Ἰησοῦ, μηδὲ λαβὼν ἀπὸ Ἰησοῦ τὴν Μαρίαν γινομένην καὶ αὐτοῦμητέ ρα: "We must dare say, then, that the first-fruits of the entire Scriptures are the gospels; but among the gospels, the first-fruits is the one according to John; for no one can come to an understanding of it [τὸν νοῦν . . . λαβεῖν, literally "grasp its mind"], unless he recline upon Jesus' breast [στῆθος] and unless he receive from Jesus Mary to become his mother."

4. In the Vulgate, *in sinum Patris*; the accusative here in both the Greek and the Latin (where one might expect to find, as in 13.23, the dative in Greek and ablative in Latin) may have been employed by the sacred author to stress the dynamism and eternity of the relation, as also in 1.1, *apud Deum*.

For Origen, as for the living Tradition in which he shares and to which he witnesses, that "Gospel," available to the understanding of those who so recline and take Jesus' mother as their own, is a reality irreducible to any one of the texts or manuscripts of a particular evangelist, yet also somehow embodied by each. The reticence of the Fathers generally to use the term "Gospel" in the plural, a usage certainly common today, indicates their conviction that there is only one Gospel, committed to the Church in a fourfold witness.[5] Origen, drawing on Revelation 14:6, further speaks of an "eternal Gospel" (εὐαγγέλιον αἰώνιον), which he identifies as a "spiritual" (πνευματικόν) Gospel,[6] by which he seems to mean the Gospel in its fullness, analogous to the Kingdom—present now among us, but not yet fully realized, or rather fully realized in Christ, but not yet fully in us (whose effective realization in this age is the particular salvific vocation of the Church)—the "supratemporal fulfillment"[7] of the Gospel entrusted in this age to the Church and communicated in its fourfold witness. As Henri de Lubac would note, this "eternal" or "spiritual" Gospel is not a second or additional "gospel," neither is it something added materially to the evangelical kerygma nor a subsequent revelation, but rather the one Gospel communicated through the evangelists understood and grasped in its fullness because its proclamation has been fulfilled.[8]

The fourth evangelist was to become known quite early as "the theologian," in part no doubt because of his intimacy with Jesus and the depth of insight associated with the Gospel ascribed to him. A "theologian," as Evagrius of Pontus was later to aver, is "one who truly prays."[9] Like the Beloved Disciple,[10] a theologian is one who both reclines on the breast of the Lord Jesus and lives in filial relation with his Mother, herself both the perfect type of the Church in this age and the pattern of its future glory. In such a construal, the theologian must approach the Gospel contemplatively

5. See the somewhat elaborate reflection on this matter by Irenaeus, *Against Heresies*, 3.11.8, and, more recently, Hays, *Reading Backwards*; Watson, *Fourfold Gospel*.

6. Origen, *Commentary on John*, 1.7(9). See also *De principiis*, 4.3.13.

7. The term is Joseph Flipper's (see Flipper, *Between Apocalypse and Eschaton*). See also de Lubac, *History and Spirit*. For an analogous understanding of the Kingdom, see Benedict XVI, *Jesus of Nazareth I*, 46–55.

8. de Lubac, *History and Spirit*, 252.

9. Evagrius Ponticus, *Chapters on Prayer*, 60.

10. The relationship among the Fourth Evangelist, the Apostle John, and the "Disciple whom Jesus loved" has of course been the subject of considerable discussion; however, its particular resolution affects not the trajectory of these reflections.

and have been placed in a particular relationship to the Church by the Lord Jesus; in short, it is a vocation exercised in contemplative love and communion. Within the context of contemplation and communion, the Gospel is ever more deeply appropriated, and so also it is only from within this context that it can be effectively communicated and fruitfully handed on.

In his book on the baptismal vocation, the Oratorian Louis Bouyer observed—an assertion he repeated in many of his works—that "Christian truth and life" are "inseparable."[11] The contemporary division (and worse, disjunction) between theology and "spirituality," between theology and "pastoral care" is too often reflected in the compartmentalization and what one might call hyper-specialization within the theological disciplines. We are perhaps all too familiar with the phenomenon: the scholar who knows more than anyone alive about three verses in the book of Daniel, but has little understanding of how these relate to Daniel as a unity, much less the Old Testament canon or the Scriptures as a whole; or the academic whose specialization is the distinction between *ictus* and *ductus* in the use of the thurible during incensation in the Roman Rite prior to the Tridentine reform, but who has no conception of the theology of the Eucharist. This hyper-specialization fragments the experience of revealed truth,[12] a truth which is liberating precisely when and because it is lived or enacted, as Jesus suggests in concluding his night-time lesson with Nicodemus (cf. John 3:21).[13]

The best theology is that which is embodied, enacted, and inseparable from life, prayer, and ministry; it is only in this way that it can be genuinely pastoral. As Christian truth is organic, so is Christian life. An encounter with the person of Christ[14]—the starting point of Christian theology—affects not only the intellect, but the whole person. Ministerial formation in particular must keep this in mind. The *Program of Priestly Formation*, which guides seminary formation in the United States, and its companion volume crafted for lay ecclesial ministry, *Co-Workers in the Vineyard of the Lord*, speak of four pillars or dimensions of formation: human, intellectual, spiritual and pastoral. Ministerial formation is principally the integration of these

11. Bouyer, *Christian Initiation*, xxi.

12. On this, see Giussani, *Journey to Truth*.

13. Note the (quite probably) intended ambiguity of the language: ὁ δὲ ποιῶν τὴν ἀλήθειαν ἔρχεται πρὸς τὸ φῶς / *qui autem facit veritatem, venit ad lucem.*

14. One should note the centrality of *incontrare* in the thought of Giussani and *rencontrer* in the thought of Bouyer.

four dimensions. In fact, the kind of integral vision which these documents offer captures the true nature of theology as an ecclesial discipline. Grace (the "encounter") builds on nature and thus presumes the natural capacity for rational reflection and articulation, is mediated in and through community, and expresses its fruits in pastoral charity. The supernatural light of faith, the concrete, particular, praying community called the Church, and the commitment to a manner of life marked by an orientation toward and concern in love for the other are not impediments to serious theology, but in fact requisite to theology rightly understood, theology in the mode of Origen and the Fathers, St. Bernard and the monastic theologians,[15] St. Thomas, St. Bonaventure and the Scholastics, theologians such as Matthias Scheeben and John Henry Newman in the nineteenth century, as well as those of the twentieth-century theological *Ressourcement*, who nourished the mind and heart of Popes John Paul II, Benedict XVI, and Francis.

Contemplative intimacy with the Lord Jesus and a filial relationship with his Mother, synecdoche of the Church, are distinguishing features of a "theologian" in the way Origen (and arguably the entire living Tradition) construes such a life or vocation. Within this construal, to be a theologian is neither an avocation nor an occupation, an academic position or endowed appointment: it is a way of life, a manner of being in which discourse is embodied as a mode of being and relating. Much as Pierre Hadot has emphasized in reminding us of what it meant to be a "philosopher" in antiquity,[16] a theologian in this living Tradition is one who embodies his teaching (or at least strives to do so); theology is part of the fabric of an entire life and the integration of the life of study, prayer, worship, and active charity. His *vita* is the most compelling demonstration of his *doctrina*. As Origen had observed, late in his life, in responding to the criticism of Celsus:

> Now Jesus is always being falsely accused, and there is never a time when he is not being accused as long as there is evil among men. He is still silent in the face of this and does not answer with his voice; *but he makes his defense in the lives of his genuine disciples, for their lives cry out the real facts*, and defeat all false charges, refuting and overthrowing the slanders and accusations.[17]

15. The best exposition of theology in a "monastic" key is that of Leclercq, *Love of Learning and the Desire for God*. The volume's very title reveals the harmony in the monastic imagination between the life of the mind and holiness.

16. See Hadot, *Philosophy as a Way of Life*; Hadot, *What Is Ancient Philosophy?*

17. Origen, *Contra Celsum*, 4. Emphasis added.

Early Christianity was often considered by its pagan critics as a "philosophy" precisely because its adherents embraced not merely a teaching, but a manner of life that embodied that teaching; the complex of a doctrine (which is what the kerygma may have appeared to many), a manner of life, and worship (even if the particulars remained obscure to outsiders) was enough for many to consider Christianity a competing school or sect of philosophy, though no doubt a curious one. By the fourth century, as witnessed in the writings of the Cappadocians, the ascetical enterprise (whether eremitic, cenobitic, or the life of *otium honestum* embraced by Augustine and companions at Cassiciacum) was often referred to as "a life of philosophy."

The theologian is one who has entered into a *communio* with Christ in the Spirit. The governing feature of this life is relational: one is not focused on analyzing an idea, concept or abstraction (though these are necessarily employed within theological discourse), but one is in relationship with Another, *the* Other, who, even before being the object of contemplative wonder and love, is first the Subject of such an encounter and relationship.[18] No one stumbles upon God (though she may initially think she has), but rather the initiative in such an encounter is always Divine.[19] The theological life is always response to such an encounter, and is marked by gratitude, wonder, and praise. A rather touching example to this contemplative intimacy is witnessed in Origen's not infrequent use of the term "my Jesus" (ὁ ἐμός Ἰησοῦς Χριστός) when he refers to Christ,[20] whether in the more familiar discourse of preaching or in his more high-powered apologetic. Note that this intimacy is not reserved only for what might be characterized as "pastoral" activity (preaching), but is found as well in what is arguably one of Origen's most mature and intellectually demanding works. This language reflects a depth of intimacy and affection indicative of the true theologian,

18. God as the Subject of theology before he is the object of theology is one of the emphases of Jean Daniélou's provocative essay, "Les Orientations Présentes de La Pensée Religieuse," which prompted the less than irenic retort of Reginald Garrigou-Lagrange in "La Nouvelle Théologie Où Va-t-Elle?"

19. This is the perspective of Augustine, writing *Confessions* and reflecting on his past self, seeking unawares the very God who was revealing himself to Augustine in his hidden ways; the number of times he employs the adjective *arcanum* in describing the relation of God's saving activity to his own life captures this dynamic.

20. See Tzamalikos, *Origen*, especially 435–36; Tzamalikos cites *Contra Celsum* 3.31 and 3.32, Homily 20.5 on Jeremiah, as well as *Homilies* 12.1, 18.1, and 22.4 on Luke as examples. De Lubac, 63–66n90, adduces considerably more examples of this affectionate phrase in Origen's preaching.

in Evagrian terms: one who has encountered the Lord Jesus and come to love him and entrust himself to him. The theologian is one who reclines on the Lord's breast.

Yet this encounter, this contemplative relationship with the Lord, also necessarily places the theologian in a particular relationship with the Church. Perhaps a fitting way to describe that relationship is as filial. As it is by the Spirit that one is capable of acknowledging Jesus as Lord (1 Cor 12:3), and as it is by the configuration effected in baptism that one exists "in Christ" (2 Cor 5:17; Rom 6:3–5) so too it is Christ who is the way to the Father (John 14:6), granting his followers a share in his own filial relation to the Father (1 John 3:1). But this relationship with Jesus, which is constitutive of a filial relationship with God, simultaneously establishes one in a filial relationship with his Mother, synecdoche of the Church. To enjoy a contemplative relationship with the Lord is to be drawn into a relationship with his Mother. What is revealed at the foot of the Cross in the Fourth Gospel (John 19:26–27) is that the disciple whom Jesus loves must take Jesus's Mother as his own Mother; there is no discipleship which does or can relate to Jesus without at the same time relating to his Mother, understood as figure of the Church.[21] The theologian is one who has a filial relationship with the Church; this is counterintuitive in a culture bred on individual autonomy. But identity in the Scriptures and in the living Tradition of Christian praxis is never construed by some internal decision on the individual's part, but in terms of relation, by the constellation of relationships which in fact form and nurture one's identity. *Communio* is not simply an option or choice; it is how humans flourish; the original sin is the refusal of communion, the self-promotion inherent in the assertion of autonomous identity. Despite cultural and professional pressures, the theologian must avoid this temptation. Rather, he or she is one who, having

---

21. In a distinctively Christian key, figurative meanings neither destroy the type or figure (any more than the New Testament destroys the Old, *contra* the perennial Marcionite temptation in the life of the Church) nor do they render them pointless: they fulfill them. The antitype itself, in its fulfillment of the type, offers a more profound understanding of the very type, even as the type prefigures its fulfillment in antitype: for example, the Exodus of Israel from Pharaoh's grip is a type of the Paschal Mystery of Christ's death and resurrection (his Pascha), which is fulfilled in the life of the Christian in baptism. The very Mystery of Christ's own Pascha illumines the beauty and truth of Israel's Passover, it does not devalue or eliminate it. Both figure and fulfillment, type and antitype, are elements in (again, *contra* Marcionite readings) one divine economy, one divine act of loving self-communication.

encountered the Lord, now stands always in a filial relation: to Jesus's Father and to the Church as Mother.

Perhaps ministerial formation programs have suffered too long from being considered (or, worse, considering themselves) "tech" schools or programs, designed merely to impart the most effective techniques and practices under the rubric of "pastoral care." "Academic" theology is then left to graduate programs at universities. A strict division of labor is unhelpful and arguably perilous: there is no competition, much less opposition, between academic theology and pastoral care, between theology and spirituality, between contemplation and action, between serving the Church and serving the academy. If such competition or opposition is perceived, it is perhaps a sign that one has misunderstood one or both of the terms in the equation, so to speak.

Ministerial formation programs should have no fear that academic rigor or the demands of intellectual engagement are somehow a threat to ministry or pastoral care. And theologians should recognize that intellectual depth, engagement, and probity are not impaired by ecclesial sensibilities, by a rich experience of liturgical and personal prayer, or by generous pastoral activity. So-called "academic" theology may have something to learn from ministerial formation programs in which the integration of the various dimensions (human, intellectual, pastoral, spiritual) is a central emphasis, and in which ecclesial commitments and sensibility are essential features. The living Tradition—in all its richness, depth, and diversity: intellectual, spiritual, liturgical, pastoral—is in fact a "culture" into which formation immerses students rendering them more effective and fruitful in ministry. The cultures of formation which distinguish ministerial programs—whether a seminary or a lay ministry program—can, or at least should, represent theology at its most traditional: theology undertaken in *communio* with Origen, Augustine, Evagrius, Hildegard, Bernard, Thomas Aquinas, Teresa de Ávila, Francis de Sales, John Henry Newman, Dorothy Day, and the cloud of other witnesses who adorn the living Tradition, where *doctrina* and *vita* coinhere in those who recline on the breast of the Lord and who have been entrusted to the Mother of God by her Son.

11

Son and Servant of the Church

Most Rev. Kevin C. Rhoades

"Let us love the Lord our God, and let us love his Church: him as our Father, her as our Mother; him as Lord and her as his handmaiden, for we are his handmaiden's children."[1] When considering John Cavadini's service to the Church in my diocese, these words of Saint Augustine, from his commentary on Psalm 88, came to my mind. I believe they express the vision and deep conviction that inspire John Cavadini's ecclesial service as a theologian and leader in Catholic higher education.

Love for God and his Church has animated John Cavadini in his vocation as a disciple of Jesus Christ here in the Diocese of Fort Wayne–South and at the University of Notre Dame. John venerates the Blessed Virgin Mary, the namesake of the university where he serves, the handmaid of the Lord who accompanies our pilgrim Church with a mother's love. John's love for the Church naturally includes this Marian thread of devotion since she is the perfect image of the Church's role as Mother. The Church, the sacrament of God's love, finds in Mary the model of her life. John's personal devotion to Our Lady at Our Lady's university unites him to the popular devotion of the people as we humbly walk with her who teaches us to follow in the footsteps of her Son in the hope of future glory in her company.

---

1. Augustine, "Exposition 2 on Psalm 88," 302.

SERVANT OF THE LOCAL CHURCH

After I was installed as Bishop of Fort Wayne-South Bend in 2010, I learned from my predecessor, Bishop John D'Arcy, about John's excellent work at the University of Notre Dame and his extensive service in this diocese. I already knew of his theological scholarship. Bishop D'Arcy shared with me the immense help he received from John in his ministry as bishop. The Church needs her theologians. Bishop D'Arcy shared with me the valued assistance he received from John Cavadini in exercising his teaching office. I have been blessed to receive that assistance as well.

At the same time, John would be the first to point out that this is not just a one-way street. John is acutely aware of the Catholic university's and the Catholic theologian's essential relationship to the hierarchy of the Church. He is genuinely grateful for the guidance of the Church's pastors. John recognizes that the bishop must not be seen as an external agent in the life of the Catholic university or the Magisterium as external to the work of theology. John believes in the charism entrusted by Christ to Peter and the apostles and to their successors.

John Cavadini's understanding and promotion of the Catholic identity and mission of the University of Notre Dame and his writings on the Catholic identity and mission in the Church's institutions of higher education provide a rich reflection that serves the Church's mission of evangelization. He articulates well the vocation to which faculties and administrators at our Catholic universities and colleges are called in serving the mission, what it means to be Catholic, and the inestimable service that these institutions, born from the heart of the Church, can provide in our culture today. John is an eloquent spokesman for the importance of the study of theology in Catholic university education as well as for the university's relationship to the Church as essential to its institutional identity (*Ex corde ecclesiae* 27).

Intimate to, not separate from, John's theological work, leadership in academia, and service to the Church in the United States and beyond is his active participation in this local church. John and his wife Nancy are active parishioners at Saint Matthew Cathedral Parish in South Bend. There they participate in the liturgy. There they raised their children. And there they receive the graces of the sacraments, strengthening them in their vocation as disciples, as Catholic spouses and parents, and as lay people in the world, including John's work at Notre Dame.

THE CHARITABLE VISION OF THEOLOGY AND CATECHESIS

I imagine that John's love for, and commitment to, the Church was shaped by his study of the life and teachings of Saint Augustine who experienced the Church as "the true mother of Christians" and as our teacher, the guarantor of the Scriptures. John's affection and passion for the Church reminds me of Augustine's words: "We have the Holy Spirit if we love the Church: we love the Church if we remain in her unity and charity."[2]

Like Augustine, John Cavadini's life and work is a response with humility to the call of our mother, the Church. This includes John's service to the Church in our diocese. He always responds "yes" to the bishop's call for assistance in building up the Body of Christ in our diocese. This includes his numerous talks to our priests, Catholic school educators, catechists, and others. It includes leadership or participation in conferences and other ecclesial events. It includes teaching in diocesan programs for the ongoing formation of our priests, the formation of permanent deacons, and the formation of our catechists and other lay ecclesial ministers as well as retreats, days of recollection, parish missions and events for all parishioners.

John Cavadini has worked hard to live the ecclesiology of *communio* laid out so beautifully in the Second Vatican Council's Dogmatic Constitution on the Church, *Lumen Gentium*. John's service to the universal Church is always in and through his own parish and diocese. He understands and lives the essential *communio* with his bishop, the link through which he is in communion with the universal Church which he serves. John's service to the Church begins with his presence and participation in his parish and extends to the diocese and the universal Church. John lives the *communio* he teaches in the classroom.

I wish to highlight what I believe is John's greatest contribution to the life of our local Church: catechesis. John Cavadini has been at the forefront of the renewal of catechetical ministry in the United States and in this diocese. Concurrently, he has been a strong proponent of the task of theologians in this ecclesial service. As a theologian and as past chair of the theology department at Notre Dame, John accepted and promoted the responsibility of theologians "of participating in the building up of Christ's Body in unity and truth."[3] He exemplifies the theologian's ecclesial vo-

2. Augustine, *Tractates on the Gospel of John*, 48.
3. Congregation for the Doctrine of the Faith, "Donum Veritatis," par. 40.

cation. As "faith seeking understanding," theology has importance for the Church and its mission of evangelization and catechesis.

> Theology offers its contribution so that the faith might be communicated. Appealing to the understanding of those who do not yet know Christ, it helps them to seek and find faith. Obedient to the impulse of truth which seeks to be communicated, theology also arises from love and love's dynamism. In the act of faith, man knows God's goodness and begins to love Him. Love, however, is ever desirous of a better knowledge of the beloved. From this double origin of theology inscribed upon the interior life of the People of God and its missionary vocation, derives the method with which it ought to be pursued in order to satisfy the requirements of its nature.[4]

As a theologian, John Cavadini's commitment to the renewal of catechesis exemplifies the vocation of theologians to the communication of the faith. The Catholic theologian is a member of the Church and his/her freedom is exercised within the faith of the Church, not apart from or opposed to that faith. John's commitment to theology includes a commitment to catechesis, not as a limitation on academic freedom properly understood, but as a service to the Church's mission of evangelization. John also recognizes and promotes the notion that "the commitment to theology requires a spiritual effort to grow in virtue and holiness."[5]

In its message for the Year of Faith in 2012, the International Theological Commission, of which John was then a member, wrote that "theology exists only in relation to the gift of faith. It presupposes the gift of faith and endeavors to demonstrate its 'boundless riches' (Eph 3:8) both for the spiritual joy of the whole community of believers and as a service to the Church's evangelizing mission."[6] This statement captures the vision of John Cavadini regarding the relationship between theology and catechesis.

Back in 2004, in an article that *Commonweal Magazine* entitled "Ignorant Catholics," John called for "a renewed pedagogy of the basics" across all the Church's educational projects and institutions. He expressed his hope that "a renewed pedagogy of the basics will obviate the old dichotomy between catechesis and theology. Although it will make theology more

---

4. Congregation for the Doctrine of the Faith, "Donum Veritatis," par. 7.

5. Congregation for the Doctrine of the Faith, "Donum Veritatis," par. 9.

6. International Theological Commission, "Message of the International Theological Commission."

catechetical, it extends the reach of the basics into an academically rigorous theological realm."[7]

In that same article, John offered another proposal that has produced much good fruit for this diocese: "partnerships between Catholic universities and colleges and the local churches." John wrote: "Nothing will benefit the Church's ability to pass on the faith more than smart, idealistic young people, both women and men . . . well trained in the basics of the faith and in the habit of theological reflection, serving as agents of renewal in catechetical pedagogy."[8] Thanks to John Cavadini, the partnership between this diocese and the University of Notre Dame through the theology department and the McGrath Institute for Church Life, led by John for two decades, has brought a great renewal of catechesis and faith formation in the Diocese of Fort Wayne–South Bend.

In this diocese, almost all of our high school theology teachers have obtained an MA degree in theology from Notre Dame, thanks to the efforts of John Cavadini and the generosity of Our Sunday Visitor. These teachers in our diocesan high schools have been formed and educated with the "renewed pedagogy of the basics" advocated by John. Their excellent theological formation at Notre Dame and their cultivated zeal for evangelization have had a tremendous impact on the faith lives of our high school students. Thankfully, this program is now open to other diocesan employees and volunteers serving the Church in adult catechesis and faith formation and other ministries. This has been, and continues to be, an effective instrument for the new evangelization and formation of missionary disciples in this diocese.

THE GIFT OF THE MCGRATH INSTITUTE
FOR CHURCH LIFE

The McGrath Institute for Church Life provides a great service to the Church in the United States, including this diocese. Inspired by John Cavadini's vision and directed by him, the Institute, in collaboration with the academic departments and schools of the University of Notre Dame, has been at the forefront of authentic Church renewal through its online theology program, its dynamic Echo program forming leaders in faith formation, its Center for Liturgy, and its Notre Dame Vision conferences each

7. Cavadini, "Ignorant Catholics."
8. Cavadini, "Ignorant Catholics."

summer for high school students and campus and youth ministers, among other programs and initiatives. The Diocese of Fort Wayne–South Bend has benefited from all these programs of the Institute for Church Life, as John Cavadini always includes this diocese as a participant recipient in these programs. I am immensely grateful for the spiritual and pastoral renewal taking place in our parishes and schools as a result of participation in the services offered by the Institute for Church Life. I am also grateful for John's engagement of so many hundreds, actually thousands, of Notre Dame students through the years in the Church's mission. The education and training they receive through the McGrath Institute for Church Life has impacted their lives of faith and, through them, the lives of so many others to whom they have gone as missionary disciples.

Because of John Cavadini, the problem of theological and catechetical illiteracy is being addressed. I see this here in the Diocese of Fort Wayne-South Bend. As so many lament these days the loss of young adults in the Church, we are also seeing a growing number of committed young Catholics here in this diocese, educated and formed by the theology department and the McGrath Institute for Church Life at Notre Dame. I am grateful to John, and his collaborators and coworkers, for their commitment to serve the Church in this diocese and beyond. They truly consider Notre Dame's relationship to the Church as "essential to its institutional identity."[9] And, as Saint Pope John Paul II stated: "as such, it participates most directly in the life of the local Church in which it is situated" as well as participating and contributing to "the life and mission of the universal Church."[10]

In *Ex corde ecclesiae,* John Paul II wrote the following:

> By its very nature, each Catholic University makes an important contribution to the Church's work of evangelization. It is a living institutional witness to Christ and his message, so vitally important in cultures marked by secularism, or where Christ and his message are still virtually unknown. Moreover, all the basic academic activities of a Catholic university are connected with and in harmony with the evangelizing mission of the Church.[11]

John Cavadini is a leader in promoting Notre Dame's contribution to the Church's work of evangelization, especially through the McGrath

9. John Paul II, "Ex Corde Ecclesiae," par. 27.

10. John Paul II, "Ex Corde Ecclesiae," par. 27.

11. John Paul II, "Ex Corde Ecclesiae," par. 49.

Institute for Church Life. His contribution to the Church's work of evangelization in this diocese over so many years has been tremendous.

UNDER THE PATRONAGE OF SAINT JOSEPH

I began this essay with the words of Saint Augustine: "Let us love the Lord our God, and let us love his Church: him as our Father, her as our Mother; him as Lord and her as his handmaiden, for we are his handmaiden's children." I noted that these words express the conviction that inspires John Cavadini's ecclesial service. But the beautiful thing is that there is something even more to say. These words, thanks to John, now resound in the minds and hearts of thousands of young Catholics who have been taught by John at Notre Dame and in the minds and hearts of so many of the faithful in this diocese through John Cavadini and his efforts.

I mentioned earlier John's devotion to Our Lady, the image and mother of the Church which he loves. I also know of John's heartfelt devotion to her loving and most chaste spouse, Saint Joseph. Every Sunday after Mass at Saint Matthew Cathedral, he can be seen at the Saint Joseph altar in prayer, often with a grandchild or two in his arms. It seems to me quite natural that John would be devoted to Saint Joseph, not only as his example as a husband and father, John's state-in-life vocation, but also as his example in serving the Church. Saint Joseph took loving care of Jesus and Mary and, as Pope Saint John Paul II taught, "he likewise watches over and protects Christ's Mystical Body, that is, the Church, of which the Virgin Mary is the exemplar and model."[12] Saint Joseph's love and faithfulness undoubtedly inspire John in his loving service of the Church.

I know John Cavadini is a man of prayer, recognizing his need to imitate the silence of Joseph and his daily contact with Jesus in the home of Nazareth. John's daily contact with the mystery of Jesus, especially in the Holy Eucharist, certainly influences his work. Anyone who has listened to a talk by John Cavadini knows that he speaks not only from the head, but from the heart. He has encountered the One of whom he speaks. And he has learned from Joseph the readiness of will to dedicate himself to the service of Christ and His Body, the Church.

John Cavadini looks to Joseph's example and asks for his intercession in serving Christ, in serving His Mystical Body, the Church, and in serving Our Lady's University. He trusts in Saint Joseph's sure protection. I believe

12. John Paul II, "Redemptoris Custos," par. 1.

that along with Saint Augustine, Saint Joseph is John Cavadini's teacher in the service of Christ's saving mission, the mission of evangelization. Imitating the humility of Saint Joseph, John humbly serves the Lord and his Church. I am grateful that he is a member of this local Church, the Diocese of Fort Wayne-South Bend.

12

Ecclesial Theologian

Most Rev. Allen Vigneron

The theologian is not just like any other academic within a college or university but has an ecclesial dimension to his or her vocation. What are the essential markers of the ecclesial vocation of the theologian?[1]

The theologian is above all a disciple. Theology as a discipline requires an act of faith. This act of faith could be within any ecclesial communion. But for a Catholic theologian, it is communion with the Catholic Church. This relationship is not abstract but is made manifest through communion with the bishops and the Pope.

Another way to make a similar point is that the theologian has to humbly receive the object of his or her investigation. As a student of theology, I was impressed with Joseph Ratzinger in his *Introduction to Christianity*. The question that the theologian must answer is whether they profess belief in the Father, the Son, and the Holy Spirit. It's this kind of faith-filled

---

1. This contribution came about by way of an interview conducted by one of this volume's editors, Timothy P. O'Malley, then transcribed for Archbishop Vigneron, who approved the final draft. Italicized sections are O'Malley's questions, with Archbishop Vigneron's responses following. In addition to being the Archbishop of Detroit, Archbishop Vigneron completed his term as chairman of the USCCB committee on doctrine in fall of 2018 and was succeeded in the role by Bishop Kevin C. Rhoades of the Diocese of Fort Wayne–South Bend, who authored the essay immediately preceding this one.

reception that marks being a disciple, of being in communion with Christ through the Church.

Methodologically, this implies that a theologian has to take account of the Magisterium in investigating the deposit of faith. There is a need to investigate the data of Revelation. To engage in the act of positive theology before undertaking speculative theology.

How has Dr. John Cavadini's own work with the doctrine committee of the United States Conference of Catholic Bishops incarnated this ecclesial vocation?

Prof. John Cavadini is an outstanding example of the virtues as described above. Over the course of his career, John has consistently mentored graduate students in the ecclesial virtues of a theologian, all the while grounding this formation in academic excellence.

Presently, John is the longest serving member of the committee on doctrine. He brings to the deliberations of this committee strong insight relative to context of each item we discuss within the committee.

At the same time, John brings his unique scholarly awareness, his own faith-filled discipleship, to each of our deliberations. Without John, many of the conferences we've run, the manner in which we form younger theologians, would not have been on our horizon.

Dr. Cavadini has focused much of his own career on a "pedagogy of the basics," attempting to reveal the importance of Christian doctrine for ecclesial life. How would you articulate this importance today? Why is doctrine important to missionary discipleship in the Church?

Any focus on doctrine must be understood within the context of the New Evangelization. The New Evangelization presents the person of Jesus Christ. But Jesus is not just like any individual. Rather, we encounter the person of Jesus Christ through the doctrine that Jesus Christ is Lord, risen from the dead. This doctrine, reflecting on the Person of our Lord, has been developed in the history of theological thought.

Doctrine is thus always about the Person of Jesus, his message as the Word made flesh. For this reason, we can never be a "wordless" Church, focusing solely on personal experience. The claims that we make about the person of Jesus Christ is what allows us to experience an encounter with our Lord.

For this reason, doctrine is connected very closely to missionary discipleship. Doctrine is part of the Good News that we proclaim to the world. It is not a bag of wet feathers that we're burdened with. Christian doctrine is what God wants people to know in order to make them happy.

It is, thus, our responsibility to share this Good News with the world so that people can meet the "real" Christ—not some subjective fabrication. As a Church, doctrine ensures that we're offering people real salvation through Jesus Christ, not a pseudo-salvation that we have created.

You've run a variety of conferences out of the doctrine committee of the United States Conference of Catholic Bishops with Dr. Cavadini. From these conferences, what are some of the essential tasks of intellectual evangelization that must be met in today's Church?

One of the marks of our various conferences is the theme of apologetics, something that has been important to the ministry of Bishop Robert Barron. For the Church, the *intellectus fidei* (an understanding of the faith) is important for developing this apologetics.

An old apologetics had as its end the removal of obstacles. Such an approach to apologetics is still essential today. For example, one of the major obstacles to Christian faith is reductive materialism. Reductive materialism presumes that only material stuff exists. In reductive materialism, we discover a theory of evolution that isn't about the biological development of creatures. Instead, we see a bad philosophy, one in which the theory of evolution reduces the human being simply to a material object. Because of reductive materialism, we have the myth that science has superseded faith. The task of an old apologetics is to argue why there is no conflict between faith and science. It would present the roots of the conflict. What are the untenable presuppositions that led to this scientism?

A new apologetics is discernable within the writings of John Henry Newman and Maurice Blondel. Here, the task of apologetics is to demonstrate the complementarity that exists between what the heart desires and what is offered in Christian revelation. This new apologetics requires that we show how the kerygma, the Good News, the Word of Jesus Christ responds to the deepest longings of the human heart.

In essence, we need what Dr. Cavadini calls an "apologetics of love," one that combines love and conviction. Today, we too often put an antipathy between lifetime commitment and the movement of the heart to love.

Christian faith puts these together, and it is precisely this presupposition that has marked the conferences that we've run with Dr. Cavadini.

It is, in fact, one of the great delights of my work with the doctrine committee that I've come to know Dr. Cavadini as a colleague and friend. I am regularly grateful to Bishop D'Arcy for recommending him as a member of the committee. Bishop D'Arcy was right on with everything he said about Dr. Cavadini.

How do we form theologians in the future for their ecclesial vocation as theologians? As contributing to an intellectual evangelization?

One of the essentials tasks of forming theologians in their ecclesial vocation is offering them a full range of experiences appropriate to the university. Students must rigorously study. But they must also enter into the life of prayer, living out their own ecclesial vocation in the world.

Our Universities also have to make a clear distinction between religious studies and theology. Religious studies can exist within a university. But, we have to clarify that religious studies, which may be carried out without this ecclesial vocation, does not belong in the Department of Theology.

Mentorship is essential to the formation of graduate students. A University needs to hire faculty who can embody in their own lives the complementarity of a full faith commitment with an equal obligation to rigorously investigate the content of the faith.

My experience, today, is that most students have grace-filled motivations that lead them to study theology. They're bright. Those talents could have led them to lucrative careers. It's important for educators in graduate school to respect the *eros* that brought them to study in the first place. Scholarly impartiality is not betrayed because one loves Christ and the Church. As an academic and teacher myself, I've often thought about Glaucon in Plato's dialogues. A sophist, Glaucon sees his work primarily as a matter of unmasking. This tendency of Glaucon to deconstruct, to unmask, is a tendency among intellectuals today. The task of good mentorship, of an excellent graduate program in theology, is to galvanize *eros* for the intellectual life.

I suspect that this is the problem today among leadership in the theological academy. It's a bias that we have inherited from the Enlightenment. Functionally, it can't withstand the critical investigation that it insists upon. There is no pursuit that can achieve its goal without commitment.

Theologians have to be able to reveal the spuriousness of this claim. And for this reason, it's necessary to form theologians in a better grasp of philosophy from the beginning. Too often, those seeking formation in theology are deficient relative to philosophical preparation. The Church has been wise over the centuries to require the study of philosophy before theology. It's difficult to understand grace if we don't understand the nature by which grace acts. We could think about a requirement for philosophy as a concrete application of the Chalcedonian formula. The order of nature and the supernatural order are distinct but also harmonious.

A stronger philosophical formation would also allow us to speak about experience in a more nuanced way. Too often theological works speak about experience without a critical understanding of the nature of experience and judgment. Philosophy is essential here.

What kind of doctoral programs does the Church need to carry out this work?

Doctoral programs in the Church need to better articulate the issues in understanding faith in our era. These programs should prepare students to get down to the roots of the problem rather than to remain on the peripheries. These students must be formed to steer a right course between fideism and an intellectualism without *eros*. As such, the doctoral program would form the student in an appropriate philosophical erudition. They would be acquainted with the whole intellectual tradition, the entire theological heritage, coming to see how every part fits into a coherent whole. There would be something deeply Christological about their formation. They would know the work of St. Thomas Aquinas—certainly, not every theologian should be a Thomist but every theologian needs to be in dialogue with St. Thomas.

13

Abraham's Sacrifice across Abrahamic Religions

Gabriel Said Reynolds
with Rasoul Rasoulipour

In his 1964 encyclical on the Church, *Ecclesiam Suam*, Pope Paul VI includes a short yet important statement on Islam: "Then we have those worshipers who adhere to other monotheistic systems of religion, especially the Moslem (sic) religion. We do well to admire these people for all that is good and true in their worship of God."[1] With this declaration, the holy father calls on Catholics to recognize the sincerity of Islamic worship. Indeed, Catholics might observe the prayer life of Muslims, including the elements of Islamic ritual prayer (which involves ritual washing and full prostrations), as an expression of deep devotion to God. In a special way, Catholics might observe the annual Islamic pilgrimage to Mecca, with its arduous rites over multiple days, as a moment of particular devotion. At the heart of that pilgrimage is the Islamic story of Abraham, and especially the story of God's command that he sacrifice his son. The following essay and its adjoining excursus include the perspectives of a Christian and a Muslim on that story, which bear relevance for Muslim–Christian relations.

The orientation of this dialogical work reflects a conference that John Cavadini and the McGrath Institute for Church Life organized in April

---

1. Paul VI, "Ecclesiam Suam," par. 107.

2012 on the "The Church and Islam." Both contributors to this essay were participants in that conference. Cavadini asked the participants to offer a study on an inspiring personality from the other's tradition and thereby to develop a "hermeneutic of spiritual admiration." In Cavadini's vision for inter-religious dialogue, we are not to set aside our faith or theological principles in a sort of compromise. Instead we are to appreciate the theological world of another tradition, and ultimately find holiness therein. His vision is an answer to Pope Paul VI's declaration in *Ecclesiam Suam* and allows believers to engage with the other in charity while offering a witness to their own faith. This is our task in the following essay, wherein one of us (Reynolds) offers the primary essay and the other (Rasoulipour) provides an extended excursus on the question of which son Abraham was to sacrifice: Isaac or Ishmael.

THE OBEDIENCE OF ABRAHAM
BY GABRIEL SAID REYNOLDS
UNIVERSITY OF NOTRE DAME

At the heart of the binding narrative in Genesis 22 is the obedience of Abraham. The narrative opens with God's command to Abraham: "Take your son, your only son Isaac, whom you love, and go to the land of Moriah, and offer him there as a burnt offering on one of the mountains that I shall show you" (Gen 22:2, NRSV). By describing Isaac as the son "whom you love" the biblical author means to emphasize the magnitude of the test put before Abraham. Yet Abraham does not object to the command or hesitate to fulfill God's will; rather, the biblical author relates that Abraham departed for the sacrifice "early the next morning" (Gen 22:3), a detail evidently meant to emphasize his obedience. Again it is the obedience of Abraham which is highlighted in the denouement of the account:

> By myself I have sworn, says the LORD: Because you have done this, and have not withheld your son, your only son, I will indeed bless you, and I will make your offspring as numerous as the stars of heaven and as the sand that is on the seashore. And your offspring shall possess the gate of their enemies, and by your offspring shall all the nations of the earth gain blessing for themselves, *because you have obeyed my voice.*[2] (Gen 22:16–19)

---

2. Emphasis added.

At the end of her lucid reflection on the story of the sacrifice of Abraham's son in Judaism, Christianity, and Islam, Carol Bakhos notes that there are various voices in the three traditions that find the story of the near-sacrifice unsettling. She writes, "The traditions also carry with them voices, cries, whimpers, and shouts, muffled by the sweep of time, that resist the ungodly Godly command."[3] Yet each tradition has also developed particular ways to discover beauty in the story of the sacrifice of Abraham's son, a story found not only in Genesis 22 but also in Qur'an 37. The interpretive history of this story is an example of how meaning is found in the dynamic relationship of a tradition with its scripture.

As Bakhos notes, the ethical and theological questions raised by the account of the binding of Isaac in Genesis 22 were of interest already to early Jewish interpreters. Some note that the silent obedience of Abraham to which we alluded above is perplexing in light of the Genesis 18 account where Abraham argues with God on behalf of Sodom. If Abraham were willing to argue with God for the sake of others, would he not do so for the sake of his own son?[4] Some interpreters address this question by noting that nothing is asked of Abraham in Genesis 18, whereas the scenario of Genesis 22 is framed as a challenge to his obedience and his willingness to endure suffering and loss. To this point, it is significant that the larger arc of the biblical narrative is in part framed by the merits that Abraham and the other patriarchs accrued, an idea known as *zekhut avot* ("merits of the fathers"). This is reflected in the denouement of the Genesis 22 account (quoted above), which insists that Abraham's offspring (and through them the entire world!) will be blessed because of his obedience.

The focus on the obedience of Abraham, however, raises the question of the role of Abraham's son in the whole scenario. In a study of the sacrifice story in the Bible and the Qur'an, M. Shahid Alam notes that while the Bible suggests that Abraham never informed Isaac of the plan to kill him as a sacrifice, the Qur'an explicitly has Abraham consult with his son (whom Alam considers to be Ishmael, although the Qur'an never explicitly notes whether Isaac or Ishmael is intended).[5] Commenting on Genesis 22, he writes: "During the three days that they are on the road, heading for the

---

3. Bakhos, *Family of Abraham*, 210.

4. See Bakhos, *Family of Abraham*, 194.

5. See the excursus appended to the end of this essay, in which my colleague and interlocutor, the Muslim scholar Rasoul Rasoulipour, comments on the interpretation that Ishmael—rather than Isaac—is the son to be sacrificed.

sacrificial site, Abraham does not speak to his son, and, when his son questions him about the absence of the sacrificial animal, he offers an evasive if not misleading answer."[6] In contrast, in the Qur'an 37:101 has Abraham say: "'My son! Surely I saw in a dream that I am going to sacrifice you. So look, what do you think?'"[7]

Alam explains that it was a risk for Abraham to consult with his son in this way. "There is a chance that [his son] might decide that the dream is not from God or, believing it is from God, he might yet refuse to become a sacrificial victim."[8] He adds: "Yet, the Qur'anic Abraham does take this risk. He will not sacrifice his son against his will, even if he is acting in obedience to God."[9] Alam contrasts the noble act of Abraham in the Qur'an to his conduct in Genesis, which does not have him consult his son. To Alam this contrast redounds to the superior "moral economy" of the Qur'an.[10]

While Alam recognizes that Jewish exegetes were interested in precisely this question, he restricts his study to the text of scripture. Here, however, something is lost by reading scripture independently of its interpretive community. A religious tradition is not scripture alone, but rather involves the full flowering of a community's reading of its scripture. It is worth emphasizing, therefore, the many Jewish traditions that insist that Isaac was an active participant in the sacrifice of Genesis 22. Indeed, this is suggested already by a text in the Hebrew Bible, namely Judith 8:26, which relates that Isaac was "tested."[11]

Moreover, the notion that Isaac was an active participant in the sacrifice is widespread in both Targums and Jewish exegetical literature. As Bakhos notes, in works including *Targum Neofiti*, *Pseudo-Jonathan*, and *Genesis Rabbah*, Isaac asks that his father tie him for fear that his courage might fail him. *Pseudo-Jonathan* has Isaac declare to his father as they prepare for the sacrifice: "Bind me properly (aright), lest I tremble from the affliction of my soul, and be cast into the pit of destruction, and there be

---

6. Alam, "Ishmael and Isaac," 145. He comments: "'It does not appear that the narrative of the near-sacrifice in the Torah views Isaac a person [sic] endowed with autonomy."

7. A. Droge translation.

8. Alam, "Ishmael and Isaac," 146.

9. Alam, "Ishmael and Isaac," 146.

10. See also Afsar, "Comparative Study," 495.

11. "Remember what he did with Abraham, *and how he tested Isaac*, and what happened to Jacob in Syrian Mesopotamia, while he was tending the sheep of Laban, his mother's brother" (Jdt 8:26).

found profaneness in thy offering" (Gen 22:10).[12] For his part Josephus has Isaac (who is 25 years old at the time) build the altar on which he is to be sacrificed.[13] Something similar is found with the Syriac Christian homilist Jacob of Serugh (d. 521), who has Isaac assist his father in building the altar on which he would be killed. He declares: "He had seen the priest building an altar for his own sacrifice / and stretched out his hand in order to finish [the building] with him untroubled."[14]

In continuity with this Jewish line of interpretation, the idea that Isaac was a willing participant in the preparations for the sacrifice plays a particular role in the unfolding of Christian reflection on Genesis 22. From an early period Christian scholars in both the East and West read the story of the binding of Isaac typologically. To some authors, such as Melito of Sardis (d. ca. 180), the ram which is found "caught in a thicket by its horns" (Gen 22:13) and is subsequently sacrificed in place of Isaac is a type for Christ. He writes: "The ram when slain redeemed Isaac thus also the Lord when slain saved us."[15] Yet among Church fathers the opinion is also found that Isaac himself is a type for Christ. Bakhos writes: "Isaac serves as a model (typos) for Jesus, who also carries the wood on his shoulders, silently and willingly accepting his fate."[16] Augustine alludes to both typological interpretations in the *City of God*.[17]

To this end it is interesting to note that one of the few passages in the Qur'an with a sense of ransom or redemption is found at the end of the near-sacrifice tale. In 37:107, the Qur'an declares of Abraham's son: "And We ransomed him with a great sacrifice" (In Arabic: *fadaynahu bi-dhibhin 'azim*).[18] Muslim exegetes have long debated why the sacrifice is called

12. Etheridge, "Targum Pseudo-Jonathan in English."

13. See Josephus, *Jewish Antiquities*, 1:232; Bakhos, *Family of Abraham*, 199.

14. Jacob of Serugh, *On Abraham and His Types*, 90.

15. Grant, "Melitos of Sardis, Fragment of Paschal Homily," 32. Cf. Bakhos, *Family of Abraham*, 201.

16. Bakhos, *Family of Abraham*, 200.

17. "And on this account, Isaac carried the wood on which he was to be offered up to the place of sacrifice, just as the Lord Himself carried His own cross. Finally, since Isaac himself was not killed—for his father had been forbidden to kill him—who was that ram which was offered instead, and by whose foreshadowing blood the sacrifice was accomplished?" (Augustine, *City of God*, 16.32). Cf. Bakhos, *Family of Abraham*, 201.

18. The ritual slaughter at the feast of *Al-Adha* (on the tenth day of the Islamic month of Dhu al-Hijja)—which can be performed at the annual Islamic pilgrimage (*hajj*) or elsewhere—commemorates the ransom of Abraham's son (although this slaughter is generally not seen to be a sacrificial act which involves redemption).

"great" when *only* an animal was killed in the place of Abraham's son. In his commentary *Zad al-masir*, Ibn al-Jawzi (d. 1200) presents four opinions, including the idea that the animal killed in place of Abraham's son was sent from heaven.[19] More likely, the Qur'anic allusion to a "great sacrifice" reflects the symbolic value which the ransoming of Isaac had acquired in Late Antiquity.

There are some reasons to conclude, therefore, that Jewish, Christian, and Islamic traditions on the near-sacrifice are closer than a literal reading of their scriptures might suggest. In his comparative study Alam notes how Martin Luther imagined a conversation between Abraham and Isaac in which the latter tells his father, not unreasonably: "God gave me to my mother through a great miracle. How then will it be possible for the promise to be fulfilled if I have been killed? Nevertheless let us first confer about this matter and talk it over."[20] Alam comments: "Martin Luther admonishes Moses for editing out some such exchange between Isaac and Abraham from the [sic] Genesis."[21] It perhaps goes without saying that Martin Luther would not have thought of himself as admonishing Moses. More to the point, Luther is actually participating in a more ancient tradition, found among Muslims as well,[22] of elaborating on scriptural passages on the basis of theological conviction.

In sum, the account of the near-sacrifice in the Bible and the Qur'an shows how religious communities develop meaning in conversation with their scripture. Genesis 22 itself highlights the obedience of Abraham, and Qur'an 37 highlights the obedience of both Abraham and his son (who in Q 37:103 is notably set down on his forehead, in a position of submission, to be sacrificed). Jews and Christians, however, also emphasize the obedience of Abraham's son, and Christians have even understood his obedience as

19. (1) The sacrificial animal used to graze in paradise; (2) the sacrifice was done according to the religion of Abraham; (3) it was the same animal offered by Abel to God; and (4) the animal was great in size and blessing. See al-Masir, *Zad Al-Masir Fi Ilm Al-Tafsir*, 7:77–78.

20. The translation is from Gritsch, *Wit of Martin Luther*, 52. See Pelikan and Lehmann, *Luther's Wars*, 4:113. For the original German, see Luther, *Luthers Werke*.

21. Alam, "Ishmael and Isaac," 144.

22. The sort of periphrastic commentary in which Luther engages here is also quite common in Islamic tradition. To give but one not unrelated example, the Shi'ite commentator al-Tabarsi (d. 1153) relates (regarding Qur'an 37) that when Sarah learned how Abraham has almost killed her son (here it is assumed that Isaac and not Ishmael is to be sacrificed), she was struck by grief and died (although Sarah has no place in the Qur'anic account of the near-sacrifice). See Bakhos, *Family of Abraham*, 212.

prefiguring that of Christ. In other words, it is true that scripture shapes religious communities, yet it is no less true that religious communities shape their scripture.

EXCURSUS: THE SACRIFICE OF ISHMAEL
BY RASOUL RASOULIPOUR
KHARAZMI UNIVERSITY

According to mainstream Islam, Abraham was obliged to sacrifice his son, Isaac or Ishmael, in a dream. He obediently followed the command but at the last moment God sent a ram to be sacrificed instead. The Holy Quran narrates the story:

> When the boy was old enough to work with his father, Abraham said, "My son, I have seen myself sacrificing you in a dream. What do you think?" He said, "Father, do as you are commanded and, God willing, you will find me steadfast." When they had both submitted to God, and he had laid his son down on the side of his face, We called out to him, "Abraham, you have fulfilled the dream." This is how We reward those who do good—it was a test to prove [their true characters]. We ransomed his son with a momentous sacrifice. (Qur'an 37:102–107)

This story created an important ritual in the Islamic Pilgrimage (Hajj). Then, all pilgrims in their annual pilgrimage to Mecca sacrifice a ram on the tenth day of their pilgrimage. They also symbolically throw seven stones at a pillar which represents Satan to recall the story in which Satan was convincing Abraham to not do whatever he had seen in the dream.

The Narration

The holy Quran confirms that Abraham in his dream saw that he would slaughter his son; however, it never mentions the name of Abraham's son as either Isaac or Ishmael! According to some traditions, Abraham saw this dream three times. Though Abraham eventually became convinced of sacrificing his son, some scholars believe that even after three times seeing the same dream Abraham still hesitated and became convinced only after receiving a revelation from Allah.[23]

23. al-Razi, *Mafatih Al-Ghayb*, 346.

For doing God's command, he took his son to the altar. The son asked his father to cover his face, also to tie his feet. Abraham did the first not the second.[24] He tried a couple of times to cut the son's neck but Gabriel did not permit the knife to work. Ultimately, he heard the message that "O Abraham! You have fulfilled the vision" and then God sent a ram to be sacrificed instead of the son.

Meanwhile, Satan tried his best to dissuade Abraham to accomplish his job. Moreover, some Shiite sources narrate that an old man (maybe the devil himself) challenged Abraham when he realized that Abraham intended to slaughter his son. He said to Abraham, "Why do you want to slaughter your son?" Abraham responded that he was to obey God's command. The old man said: "Alleluia! You intend to slaughter your son who never sinned in his short time of his life?" Abraham said that he has seen this in his dream. The old man replied that it must have been a Satanic dream. "You are the leader of the community and if you do this, others will do it!" Abraham did not continue this conversation.[25]

Which Son?

In the Quran it is not clear whether the sacrificed son was to be Isaac or Ishmael. The narrations in the Shiite sources say, however, that the sacrificed son was Ishmael for sure; whereas the narrations from the Sunni sources are split: some mention Ishmael and others mention Isaac. Muhammad Hossein Tabataba'i (d. 1981) in his well-known commentaries (*Al-Mizan*) on the holy Quran cites al-'abari's (d. 923) history who says that the early scholars of the community of our Prophet Muhammad differed on this issue. Some held that that it was Isaac while the others say it was Ishmael. Tabataba'i insists that there is no authentic narration in al-Tabari's words and argues that according to the Quran it was Ishmael who was to be sacrificed.[26]

24. Kulayni, *Al-Kafi*, 208.

25. Ibn Abu Hatam, *Tafsir Al-Qur'an Al-'Azim*, 3222.

26. Tabataba'i, *Tafsir Al-Mizan*, 1:294.

14

Eschatological Vision
Between Compromise and Intransigence

FRANCESCA ARAN MURPHY

IN THIS PAPER, I contend that the only attribute that can rescue a Catholic from intransigence or compromise in political affairs is eschatological vision. I begin by sketching what I mean by 'political matters.' Political affairs do not only happen in Washington, DC, or at the Palace of Westminster. As we know, they can take place in Florida and Tennessee and all over America. Politics is what happens whenever people argue about how to direct and govern a social organization, whether it is a business or a university or a local club. All those who make their living by teaching belong to professional associations. These associations likewise have their politics, their donkeys, their dissidents, and their leaders.

It seems much better to set one's sights by speaking about the 'office politics' known to all who work, because it gives us a focus on what can actually be achieved. The more purely 'political' and abstract our conception of politics is, the more unrealistic our expectations of what can be gained through it. People speak of political goals for their country that they would never dream of putting on the agenda for a meeting of their own co-workers.

Political leadership is where people give a steer to social organizations, small or great. And it's best to imagine forms of political leadership in which professors and teachers could actually be involved. We could all be local leaders, of some kind, so long, it seems as we don't try to make catastrophically heavy weather out of it. But then we may wonder how the prospective leaders within a university faculty or of a women's choir are supposed to be endowed with 'eschatological vision.'

How could Catholics possibly get involved in local let alone national politics if they lumber themselves with an eschatological vision? Is the advocacy of an 'eschatological vision' a sleight of hand intended surreptitiously to seduce Catholics into political quietism? Surely the only way to ensure that the light of truth is out from under the bushel, and that there is leaven in the loaf, and plenty of salt too, is to train Catholics for leadership in politics great and small? Wouldn't we rather that political affairs have Catholic leaders than any other kind?

Alas, though, one would really rather not: it is a sound and historically well-informed principle that antics of Catholics in the public square are an embarrassment to their co-religionists. By and large, therefore, Catholics who know a bit of history would greatly prefer not have to observe their co-religionists in the public square. For they commonly make obstreperous fools of themselves, and sometimes collude to play the knave into the bargain. When it comes to politics, the two great temptations into which Catholics rush like Gadarene swine are compromise and intransigence.

Compromise and intransigence are the commonest Catholic reactions to our political condition, which is most often one that could be labelled 'occupation.' More often than not, politics for us takes place within institutions or realms that have been conquered and occupied by alien powers. Mostly, not always, but by and large, we Christians live in occupied territory. The Babylonian captivity was not just one of the series of political disasters that befell ancient Israel, but, more than that, it is a working parable for many of the situations in which we operate our political strategems.

Another, more optimistic way of putting this is to say that, beyond the Church itself, Catholics cannot hope to form 'Christendom clubs,' or 'Christendom Universities,' or 'Christendom States or Countries.' Even where the Church is established by law, it will fight constantly, and we hope, valiantly, to preserve its identity, and constantly find itself a 'prisoner' or a 'captive' of powerful, worldly interests. For a small example, the Church is, as it were, the legal establishment in any Catholic educational institution, and most people who teach in Catholic schools and colleges would say that it is a daily fight to contain the operations of worldly captains of State. Beyond the Church, with its own laws and character, there is here below no 'nation' or city that can be characterized purely and simply as 'Godly' or 'God-bound.' Catholics, some of them statesmen, operate outside their own territory, and have no turf to call their own.

When he called Christians 'resident aliens,' Stanley Hauerwas was giving an optimistic, American version of the thesis of Augustine about the political Babylonian captivity of pilgrim earthlings. Cain founded the City of Man and Abel, in his short stay on earth, established the City of God, and "Scripture tells us that Cain founded a city, whereas Abel, as a pilgrim, did not found one. For the City of the saints is up above, although it produces citizens here below, and in their persons the City is on pilgrimage until the time of its kingdom comes."[1] The 'City of God' has many citizens, here below, but no city to call its own. They are God-bound travelers. These pilgrims are not landlubbers but sailors. The 'ark' of Noah is one of their symbols, because a boat is not a stable, rooted and motionless domicile, but merely a vessel for a journey.[2]

The Catholic Compromiser and Intransigent both kick against the pricks of occupancy. The Compromiser thinks shrewdly to outwit the occupying powers by pretending to go along with him. He puts on such a good show of pretending to go along with the enemy that its actually very difficult to tell if he's left off pretending. For Catholics, *compromise* in political leadership is making the best of a bad job, whilst entertaining the delusion that one is adding the salt of virtue to people and situations that are invincibly armored against salt or leaven or all the rest. One large scale example of compromise is the 'Vichy' bargain struck by Marshall Petain in 1941. 'Vichy' has become a common-place metaphor for collusion, and with some justice. The 'Vichy' compromise rests on the illusion that foreign occupation by alien powers can be ameliorated and even swung round to support some good causes, if only some sound men, like one's own team, are there to collude with the devils. A smaller scale example, closer to home, is the way in which our managerialist culture has begotten armies of administrators, who have over-run our universities and distorted their operation and ends.

1. Augustine, *City of God*, XV.1. I use the 1972 edition of this text throughout.
2. Augustine, *City of God*, XV.26.

People get into the game of collusion when we tell ourselves that this or that 'board' or directorate sets bad goals for an institution, but at least if we are on it, there will be one sound Catholic there to lead the opposition. Someone has to get onto the board, to represent the counter-position. It's the temptation of power, covering itself up with the illusion of having a good influence on people who are in fact soon to influence and corrupt us, and not vice versa. Catholics are led into such situations of political compromise by trying to find 'common ground' with bad political protagonists who despise our faith. Our Babylonian overlords want more than anything else gently to compel us to treat our faith as if it were extrinsic to our actual political aims and purposes. Our faith can never be entirely outside of our political aims, though these ends may touch the faith only indirectly and tangentially.

The brigade of Catholic political Intransigents is better known to us, because many of them have been theologians of one kind or another. The Intransigent is the man of principle with the impossible plan, the plan that it is politically impossible to implement. The Intransigent will brook no compromise, and broker no deals with their opponents and overlords. Noah Rothman has written an entertaining study of intransigency in contemporary American politics, noting that both progressivists and conservatives have lately succumbed to political fatalism, as a result of 'unrealistic expectations.' Imagining that 'change should happen because we will it,' can only lead to despair and a 'weakness for extremism,' which is another way of saying, a weakness for giving up on political process.[3] For Christians, the political process consists in negotiating with, out-maneuvering, and outwitting the Babylonian conquerors.

The intransigents have done more in the past half century to betray Catholic schools and universities than all of the compromisers and all of the non-believers combined. For they simply cannot put their hands to working with the actually existing people in the actually existing political situations in which they find themselves. Repeatedly the Intransigent captain sinks his own little ship of state, scuttling and capsizing the little boat—it seems too damnable to him to be worth bailing out. The Intransigent can always think of a better ship of state than the one he is in, which is OK, except for that no craft would be better without the faith to steer her home, in the dark, by the stars. Casting themselves as angels of light, they cannot focus a charitable eye upon their peers and co-workers. They cannot extract the

3. Rothman, "Fatalist Conceit."

moat in their brother's lens because of the beam in their own eye, certainly, but they also cannot see the beams of light in their weaker brethren for the dust storm that rages around their own heads. Thousands upon thousands of idea particles whirl around the Intransigent's head, a perfect perichoretic swarm of specks, motes and plain dust, which renders it impossible for the Intransigent to use a situation to Catholic and Christian advantage, to trade horses with his opponents, or to cooperate peacefully in the pursuit of common aims.

Neither the Compromiser nor his bed-fellow the Intransigent can succeed in political engagement, neither can bring the Gospel to bear in the public square, because neither Obdurate nor Pragmatist can imagine their political society as a 'corpus mixtum,' a body of people in which good and evil are inextricably mixed together, or at least mixed so thoroughly that only a harvesting angel out of the Book of Revelation could extricate the one from the other. This sounds counter-intuitive, because the zealous Intransigent may be a bit of a civic dualist and a political Manichee, but the Compromiser seems born to lead some 'Corpus mixtum,' in which, as Saint Augustine interprets our Lord's parable, the wheat and the tares are tangled up like spaghetti until the end of time.[4]

Augustine presents the 'corpus mixtum' idea early in the *City of God*. It pops up in the first book already, where Augustine claims that,

> [The Church] must bear in mind that among these very enemies are hidden her future citizens; and when confronted with them she must not think it a fruitless task to bear with their hostility until she finds them confessing the faith. In the same way, while the City of God is on pilgrimage in this world, she has in her midst some who are united with her in participation in the sacraments, but who will not join with her in the eternal destiny of the saints. . . . At one time they join his enemies in filling the theatres, at another they join with us in filling the churches. But, such as they are, we have less right to despair of the reformation of some of them, when some predestined friends, as yet unknown even to themselves, are concealed among our most open enemies. In this, those two cities are interwoven and intermixed in this era, and await separation at the last judgement.[5]

4. Augustine, *City of God*, XX.9.

5. Augustine, *City of God*, X.35.

Augustine is never more uncompromising, never more judgmental, never more the partially-reformed Manichean, never more prophetic, than when he writes of about the 'corpus mixtum.' It takes the *most* eschatological perspective to imagine a political society as the intermingling of two citizenries, two opposed armies, one headed to perdition and the other destined for eternal paradise. To see your own society, your own university or club, or business, as a 'corpus mixtum,' one must, in imagination, stand posed above it in space and in time, and see it, as from a spaceship, or as Saint John the Divine saw human history swirling to its end from a vantage point in 'eschatological time.' It takes a purely eschatological perspective to see one's own civic world as peopled by demonic opponents, some of whom are predestined to conversion into allies, and by seeming soul mates, some of whom are false friends indeed. Only an eschatological vision can make one see, on the one hand, that some of one's colleagues are citizens of Babylon, and some of the heavenly Jerusalem. The gift of the perception of radical evil and radical good in the ordinary human beings around us, and both of them mixed and intermingled, is the eschatological vision. And this judgmental, shrewd vision is what it takes to exercise successful Catholic political leadership, in matters great and small.

The Christian statesman is the Eschatological Statesman. In matters small and great, the Eschatological Statesman is a descendant of the hirsute prophets of the Old Testament. It is perhaps not quite true that John the Baptist is the last of the line of Old Testament prophecy, for the eschatological statesmen continue to declare with stony, pitiless eyes that the 'axe is laid to the root.' Charitable to a fault in reckoning with individual men and women, the Christian leader who has inherited prophetic blood loathes to yield an inch on matters of principle. Prophetic blood is like Flannery O'Connor's 'wise blood' in this, that it engenders an instinctual and unerring feel for the weight and balance of situations. The Christian statesman can smell a rat, and an opportunity, and a threat.

This is not to say that he can always gauge, in practical terms, the gravity of the threat: like his biblical forebears he consistently exaggerates the dangers, and foresees bleak devastation and the coming of the Lord's Day in setbacks too paltry to make the secular history books. The Eschatological Statesman seldom chills, in matters of state, and never lets things pass, or imagines he can muddle through. He knows that he and his fellow citizens of the new Jerusalem are never in less than mortal danger of being wasted by the enemy. So he seldom chooses his battles with caution aforethought.

He often has to be talked down from the ledge by the cabinet of donkeys and dissidents no prophet can do without. The Eschatological Statesman sees storm clouds brewing under the bluest and most apparently innocent skies.

And this is how this Noah keeps the ship of state afloat: he violently over-estimates every peril, and for that very reason he fights with every last breath for the survival of his ark. While the bystanders looked on mockingly, in broad daylight and sunshine, Noah had built that ark; with not a cloud in the sky he hacked down trees and sawed planks, and hammered and poured on pitch; on the sunniest spring day he drove his protesting wife, with Shem, Ham and Japheth in tow, and their little ones, and all the livestock he could collect, up the wooden drawbridge and into the ark of safety. How they laughed, those bystanders who were soon to drown in the flood. How they cried as the Lord God unleashed thunder, tempests and downpour from the skies.

Like the Intransigent, no less, Noah had a crazy, utopian plan; but unlike the political incompetent, the eschatological captain of state sweated, and toiled with hopeful craftsmanship to make his crazy idea a reality. In the mid-summer sun he wanted to build a ship to rescue a remnant of humanity and a good spread of animals from an imminent, cosmic disaster movie; driven by vast waves in his little wooden tub, with the flood gates of heaven opening upon him, Noah the just man, the man of faith, still aimed to rescue his remnant from the deathly waves.

Even the mature, episcopal Augustine was a little impatient with this childish, nautical turn in the Genesis narrative, urging that "only a love of disputation would allow anyone to contend that the elaborate details of the historical narrative are not symbols designed to give a prophetic picture of the Church."[6] The elaborate details about the construction of the Ark are surely there, in part, to show the reader that Noah, both as ship-wright and as involuntary sailor, carries out God's command meticulously and with ridiculous exactitude, as a just man, who is absolutely determined to rescue his tiny, querulous remnant. He does not rescue his remnant because they are likeable, and certainly not because they are righteous people like him. Long before Augustine allegorized his sea voyage, Noah saw and smelt, that "the clean and the unclean are contained" in the "unity" of the Ark.[7]

6. Augustine, *City of God*, XV.27.
7. Augustine, *City of God*, XV.27.

Christian, eschatological statesmanship is a kind of mean between collaboration and intransigence, though not a split down the middle, rationalist kind of mean, but rather a charismatic, baptized in the Spirit and in fire, kind of Aristotelian mean. Eschatological statesmanship does not simply 'drive down the middle of the road' between lukewarm pragmatism and meretricious dedication to true but irrelevant principles. It is a mean, but can be seen as synthesizing the virtues of both extremes only from high above both, from the eschatological, biblical perspective. Like the dystopian statesmanship of the compromisers, but more genuinely, it hopes and takes care to include all, clean and unclean, or as many as can be squeezed into the Ark. Like the utopian statesmanship of the intransigents, it is a stickler for principles, only, in this case, for principles that matter and can be applied in this historical situation.

Where it differs most sharply from the world-weary, yet worldly, pragmatist and the unworldly, but not very supernatural zealot, is that the Christian, eschatological vision of politics, great and small, is not based on morality. When our Lord drove the merchants out of the temple, it was not with a moral yardstick. Our Lord's righteous anger was fueled by the degeneration of Jerusalem's house of worship into a market. It was not a matter of moral disapproval of salesmanship, but of eschatological condemnation of the perversion of the Temple worship by the very implements of sacrificial worship, the animals. It was not a mere moral disapproval of the financial transactions, the coin-exchange and sale of pigeons and lambs, but a prophetic denunciation of the denaturing of the house of prayer, worship and sacrifice by the very means of worship. The crime was not moral but religious, the turning of worship from service to God to service of human appetite. It was the re-orientation of heaven bound gifts into merchandise that provoked the wrath of God.

Likewise, Augustine's vision of the two branches of humanity, "those who live by human standards" and "those who live by God's will" is not based on mere moral disapproval of the human society which is "doomed to undergo eternal punishment with the devil" or moral approval of those "predestined to reign with God for all eternity."[8] Augustine's vision of history as the two, entangled paths of the City of Man and the City of God is not a moralizing vision, but a biblical, prophetic vision of history, a metahistorical extension of a reading of the biblical narrative into the whole of human civilization. From Paleolithic Cain and Abel until the end of

8. Augustine, *City of God*, XV.1.

time, the City of Man and the City of God will forge their spiraling, paths, writing variants on the same human story over and over again. The moralizing Compromiser or Intransigent thinks of Cain's City first and foremost as immoral. But it seeks its own goods; it is not sound political strategy to conceive of political disagreements as conflicts between moral rectitude and absence of morality. They are religious disagreements.

The citizens of the worldly city worship that very city as their mirror image. The political motto of that city is Lenin's 'who whom?', who is doing what to whom? Since the citizens of the heavenly city worship not themselves but another, it is not surprising that their political leaders conceive their task not as self-aggrandizement but as service to others. How will compromisers and intransigents offer genuine service to the common good? Eschatological faith is given to only a few of us, but all of can serve in our local public squares. The eschatological leader will press-gang into his service those folks who, by themselves, are politically rudderless: the compromisers become his donkeys, and the intransigents make very useful dissidents under the guidance of a good strategical thinker. He cannot function without a war cabinet of such folks, who here prove their worth. The eschatological leader is not always a saint, or, at least, he is like nearly every saint, and has the vices of his virtues. It can scarcely be denied that, so single-minded is he, so absorbed is he in his task of service, and so determined that others, too, shall serve the ends of the City, that every one of his social interactions is oriented toward furthering the good of the City. Every encounter is an encounter with the general, directing his troops here and there.

It seems as if, for Augustine himself, history *is* nothing more or less than the interplay of the two cities. He tells us that, "My task is to discuss . . . the rise, the development and the destined ends of the two cities, the earthly and the heavenly, the cities which we find interwoven in this present transitory world, and mingled with one another."[9] Having set himself that task, he chronicles the adventures of man from Adam up to Theodosius, and thence down to the sacking of Rome by the Goths in 410 AD. So it seems as if history emerges from the friction between the two cities. Why else are the two societies interwoven, except to produce some fruit or offspring?

That, at least, is Kant's kind of creative misreading of this ancient Christian trope: it might be that when Kant claims that higher civilizations emerge out of conflict and war amongst men, he has some bodged,

9. Augustine, *City of God*, XI.1.

muddled memory of the ancient Christian trope of the two cities at the back of his mind. From Kant's "creative mis-recollection"[10] of Augustine, then, arise the idea of some kind of 'dialectic' as the motor of history, that is, the idea that history, and higher and more sophisticated and even utopian human civilizations emerge out of the crucible of war.

But that is not exactly what Augustine had in mind. God's original intention, he says, was the unity and fraternity of the human race. We may imagine that, for the proper interpretation of original sin to be possible, God had little alternative outside a monogenetic creation of the human race: unless God made humanity from a single man, God would have made it impossibly difficult for theologians to explain the universal extent of original sin. But no, according to Augustine's reading of God's mind on this point: "God chose to make a single individual the starting point of all mankind, and that his purpose in this was that the human race should not merely be united in a society by natural likeness, but should be bound together by a kind of tie of kinship to form a harmonious unity, linked together by the 'bond of peace.'"[11]

It was, as it seems, first the Fall and then the rescue, and the delivery of undeserved grace, to some of humanity, that drove the wedge between the two societies. For, under the impulse of grace, some elect to live "by the standard of the spirit," whilst others capitulate to the law of death in their members, and live "by the standard of the flesh."[12]

It follows, then, that, because the two societies live by different standards, each has its own idea of 'peace.' Peace is the cessation of purposeful motion, or coming to rest at the chosen end of one's journey. For the denizens of the City of Man, peace is some kind of treaty between physical needs and physical appetites: the human city aims to find rest and peace in the fulfillment of appetite, or at least its cessation. When appetite ceases to itch and generate more physical needs, then an individual has his own worldly, humanistic peace. Peace for the individual member of the City of Man is the satiation of greed, through some kind of compromise between needs and appetites; and since the City of Man as a whole, in all its members, is driven by love of self, by self-will, so peace within the worldly city as

---

10. Cyril O'Regan has put this word into our urban dictionaries, with *Anatomy of Misremembering*.

11. Augustine, *City of God*, XIV.1.

12. Augustine, *City of God*, XIV.1.

a whole is a compromise between the lusting greedy wills of all the members. This is what Augustine calls the 'peace of Babylon.'

Citizens of the 'city above,' the heavenly Jerusalem aim to come to rest, or peace, in a harmony between their own, obedient will and the will of God: the citizen of the New Jerusalem longs to say, with Dante, "in his will is our peace."[13] Peace is the right relation between ourselves and God, who is unseen above, so peace is a matter of faith, not sight. So Augustine states that, "so long as he is in this mortal body," the Jerusalemite passport holder, "is a pilgrim in a foreign land, away from God; therefore he walks by faith not by sight. That is why he views all peace, of body or of soul, or of both, in relation to that peace which exists between mortal man and immortal God, so that he may exhibit an ordered obedience in faith in subjection to the everlasting Law."[14]

So in the City of Man, 'peace' is compromised between billions of 'self-willing' wills, whereas the peace of the New Jerusalem consists in faithfully binding one's own will to the will of God. How surprising then to learn that "we," we members of this New Jerusalem, "also make use of the peace of Babylon."[15] It seems impossible to deny this without quixotic political irresponsibility. Augustine in his own time most likely was thinking of how the Gospel had spread through the pax Romana, and how very much the safety and the flourishing of Christians depended upon that worldly 'pax.' In our own time, we have only to look at what happens to the members of the Christian churches in the places where worldly, 'Babylonian,' civilization has broken down, as in parts of the Middle East, to see that we, too, must literally collude at the deepest level with the 'earthly peace' and with its values and aims. The development of civilization, it seems, is not the friction between the two cities, not their dialectic, but their 'union,' the re-union of all humanity in the embrace of the City of Man by the more wily City of God, which cannot survive on earth without its ugly brother. And it is this collusion, so it seems, which the Christian statesman must serve.

But it seems then that the Christian statesman must be a compromiser. In matters local and universal, he will have to negotiate with and harness the self-will, ambition and greed of the Babylonians in order to preserve the denizens of the City of God here below. We 'pilgrims' may have our eyes on the city above, the 'heavenly city,' but our survival on earth, so it

13. Dante Alighieri, *Paradiso*, III.85.
14. Augustine, *City of God*, XIX.14.
15. Augustine, *City of God*, XIX.26.

seems, depends on collusion with the earthly city. 'We also make use of the peace of Babylon' is likely the mantra mumbled by the bean-counters as they trade the peace of God for a bit of human pax.

The Compromiser thinks to pay the price of the worldly peace so that he, and the weaker brethren, can enjoy the thought of the pious heavenly peace. This, he fondly believes, is rendering unto Caesar what is Caesar's and unto God what is God's. He knows that Saint Paul enjoins the Romans to "be subject unto the higher powers" (Rom 13:1) and that Augustine envisages the citizens of heaven as enslaved prisoners of the Emperor who "must needs make use of this peace also, until this mortal state, for which this kind of peace is essential, passes away. And therefore, it leads . . . a life of captivity in this earthly city as in a foreign land . . . and yet it does not hesitate to obey the laws of the earthly city."[16]

But the compromising Catholic statesman, who makes his peace with Babylon, for the sake of the multitudes weaker brethren, of course, cannot actually make his compromise work. Where there is no vision, the peace perishes. The Compromiser is ultimately a dualist, like his confrere the Intransigent. He can see worldly peace, and pay a price for it, and he can see heavenly peace. He may know quite painfully, and realistically, how ugly the price of the Babylonian peace is, and what vices must be sown amongst the virtuous faithful in order to foster the bargain. The Compromiser is a realist, and knows precisely what lusts, rapacious appetites, and violences he tolerates so that his pilgrims can set their pious hearts on the heavenly city.

What he does not know how to do is to imagine, and so to create, what Augustine calls the 'harmony' between the two cities. Only the Eschatological Statesman will strike such a bargain that the treasures of the Pax Romana are brought into the new Jerusalem. For the Eschatological Statesman, by contrast, everything is caught up in the vision of the Heavenly Kingdom, and everything can be, at a stretch, related to it. The eschatological leader makes that stretch. He does not compromise and downplay the polarity between Babylon and Jerusalem, nor does he insist on their reciprocal repulsion. Rather than polarizing the two cities, he instantiates a creative polarity, or mobile analogy between the dynamic duo. Even the Babylonian peace can be imagined as an analogous relationship to the only genuine and authentic peace, in God. The Eschatological Statesman, with his prophetic faith and hopeful imagination, is the only politician who can

16. Augustine, *City of God*, XIX.17.

orient the necessary and inevitable bargain with Babylon toward the true and authentic peace.

Babylon itself is Babylon: it cannot be 'baptized' or turned into the New Jerusalem. But its worldly kind of peace of balanced human wills can be envisaged as a *relation*, an orientation toward the heavenly peace of harmony between divine and human will. The immanent earthly peace is a relationship amongst human wills, each damping down its own lust to dominate power for the sake of peace, and likewise the transcendent, heavenly peace is the loving and obedient relationship of the human will to God. The Eschatological Statesman can orient the first, immanent relationship toward the higher, transcendent relation because he can *imagine* even this relation as an analogue of the harmony between God and man. This is because, to cite the same passage over, he "views all peace, of body or of soul, or of both, in relation to that peace which exists between mortal man and immortal God, so that he may exhibit an ordered obedience in faith in subjection to the everlasting law."[17]

17. Augustine, *City of God*, XIX.14.

Selected Bibliography

Affleck-Graves, John. "Catholic Mission: Finance and Professional Schools." In *Proceedings of What We Hold in Trust Seminar*. Notre Dame, IN: McGrath Institute for Church Life, 2009.

Afsar, Ayar. "A Comparative Study of the Intended Sacrifice of Isaac/Ishmael in the Bible and the Qur'an." *Islamic Studies* 46.4 (2007) 483–98.

Alam, M. Shalid. "Ishmael and Isaac: An Essay on the Divergent Moral Economies of the Qur'ān and the Torah." *Islamic Studies* 51.2 (2012) 139–54.

Augustine. *City of God*. Edited by David Knowles. Translated by Henry Bettenson. London: Penguin, 1972.

———. *City of God*. Translated by Henry Bettenson. New York: Penguin, 2003.

———. *The Confessions*. Translated by Maria Boulding. New York: Vintage, 1998.

———. "Exposition 2 on Psalm 88." In *Expositions of the Psalms*, translated by Maria Boulding, 289–302. New York: New City, 2002.

———. *Instructing Beginners in Faith*. Translated by Raymond Canning. New York: New City, 2006.

———. *Tractates on the Gospel of John*. Translated by John W. Retig. Washington, DC: Catholic University of America Press, 2002.

Bacci, Pietro Giacomo. *The Life of St. Philip Neri: Books I and II*. Edited by William Bloomfield. n.p.: Bloomfield, 2017.

Bakhos, Carol. *The Family of Abraham*. Cambridge, MA: Harvard University Press, 2014.

Balthasar, Hans Urs von. *Spirit and Fire*. Washington, DC: Catholic University of America Press, 1984.

Barr, Stephen M. "The Mathematization of Physics and the Neo-Thomism of Duhem and Maritain." *American Catholic Philosophical Quarterly* 92.1 (2018) 123–44.

———. *Modern Physics and Ancient Faith*. Notre Dame, IN: University of Notre Dame Press, 2003.

Benedict XVI. "Caritas in Veritate." Encyclical delivered in Rome, June 29, 2009. http://w2.vatican.va/content/benedict-xvi/en/encyclicals/documents/hf_ben-xvi_enc_20090629_caritas-in-veritate.html.

———. *Deus Caritas Est: God Is Love*. Boston: Pauline, 2006.

———. *Jesus of Nazareth, Part I: From the Baptism in the Jordan to the Transfiguration*. New York: Doubleday, 2007.

Berwick, Robert C., and Noam Chomsky. *Why Only Us: Language and Evolution*. Cambridge, MA: MIT Press, 2016.

BibleGateway. "Luke 2:35." https://www.biblegateway.com/verse/en/Luke%202:35.

Bouyer, Louis. *Christian Initiation*. Tacoma, WA: Cluny, 2018.

Bowen, William G. *Inside the Boardroom*. New York: Wiley, 1994.

Buckley, Michael J. *The Catholic University as Promise and Project*. Washington, DC: Georgetown University Press, 1998.

Burtchaell, James T. *The Dying of the Light*. Grand Rapids, MI: Eerdmans, 1998.

Byron, William. "Catholic Higher Education: Past and Future." In *Proceedings of What We Hold in Trust Seminar*. Notre Dame, IN: McGrath Institute for Church Life, 2009.

Carruthers, Mary. *The Book of Memory: A Study of Memory in Medieval Cultur*. 2nd ed. Cambridge: Cambridge University Press, 2008.

———. *The Craft of Thought: Meditation, Rhetoric, and the Making of Images, 400–1200*. Cambridge: Cambridge University Press, 2000.

Cavadini, John C. "Augustine: Saint of Suspicion." *Church Life Journal*. August 20, 2018. http://churchlife.nd.edu/2018/08/20/patron-saint-of-suspicion-draining-cesspit-corruption.

Cavadini, John C. "Augustine: Saint of Suspicion." Paper presented at the University of Notre Dame, October 22, 2015. Video recording. https://www.youtube.com/watch?v=rnLCNxc5wfY.

———. "A Brief Reflection on the Intellectual Tasks of the New Evangelization." *Josephinum Journal of Theology* 19 (2012) 109–20.

———. "The Church as the Sacrament of Creation: A Reading of Origen's Commentary on the Song of Songs." *Communio* 42 (2015) 89–118.

———. "Ignorant Catholics." *Commonweal*. May 12, 2004. https://www.commonwealmagazine.org/ignorant-catholics.

———. "Introductory Comments." In *Proceedings of What We Hold in Trust Seminar*. Notre Dame, IN: McGrath Institute for Church Life, 2009.

———. "Social Justice and Love in the Christian Tradition." *Church Life Journal* 1.4 (2013).

———. "Theology at a Catholic University." In *Proceedings of What We Hold in Trust Seminar*. Notre Dame, IN: McGrath Institute for Church Life, 2009.

———. "Why Study God?" *Commonweal*. September 30, 2013. https://www.commonwealmagazine.org/why-study-god.

Cavadini, John C., and Danielle M. Peters, eds. *Mary on the Eve of the Second Vatican Council*. Notre Dame, IN: University of Notre Dame Press, 2017.

Cavanaugh, William T. *Theopolitical Imagination: Discovering the Liturgy as a Political Act in an Age of Global Consumerism*. New York: Bloomsbury, 2002.

Chait, Richard, et al. *Improving the Performance of Governing Boards*. Phoenix: Oryx, 1966.

Chapman, A. D. *Numbers of Living Species in Australia and the World*. 2nd ed. Canberra: Australian Biological Resources Study, 2009.

Code of Canon Law: Latin-English Edition. Washington, DC: The Canon Law Society of America, 1983.

Congregation for the Doctrine of the Faith. "Donum Veritatis: Instruction on the Ecclesial Vocation of Theologian." Delivered in Rome, May 24, 1990. http://www.vatican.va/roman_curia/congregations/cfaith/documents/rc_con_cfaith_doc_19900524_theologian-vocation_en.html.

Conklin, Richard. "How Catholic the Faculty?" *Notre Dame Magazine*. 2007. https://magazine.nd.edu/news/how-catholic-the-faculty.

Selected Bibliography

Corson, Dorothy V. *A Cave of Candles: The Story Behind the Notre Dame Grotto*. Nappanee, IN: Evangel, 2006.

Daniélou, Jean. "Les Orientations Présentes de La Pensée Religieuse." *Études* 249 (1946) 5–21.

Dante Alighieri. *Paradiso*. Edited and translated by Robin Kirkpatrick. New York: Penguin, 2007.

de Lubac, Henri. *History and Spirit: The Understanding of Scripture According to Origen*. Translated by A. Nash. San Francisco: Ignatius, 2005.

DeFelice, Jonathan. "Faith and Academic Life." In *Proceedings of What We Hold in Trust Seminar*. Notre Dame, IN: McGrath Institute for Church Life, 2009.

Delegates of the Second Congress of Catholic Universities of the World. "The Catholic University in the Modern World." *NCEA College Bulletin* 35.3 (1973) 1–10.

Deneen, Patrick. *Why Liberalism Failed*. New Haven: Yale University Press, 2018.

Descartes, René. *Discourse on Method and Meditations on First Philosophy*. Translated by Donaled A. Cress. Indianapolis: Hackett, 1998.

Dosen, Anthony J. *Catholic Higher Education in the 1960s: Issues of Identity, Issues of Governance*. Charlotte, NC: Information Age, 2009.

Dougherty, Jude P. *The Nature of Scientific Explanation*. Washington, DC: Catholic University of America Press, 2013.

Doyle, Daniel E. "Mary, Mother of God." In *Augustine Through the Ages: An Encyclopedia*, edited by Allan D. Fitzgerald and John C. Cavadini, 542–45. Grand Rapids: Eerdmans, 1999.

Dulles, Avery. "God and Evolution." *First Things: A Monthly Journal of Religion and Public Life*. October 2007. https://www.firstthings.com/article/2007/10/001-god-and-evolution.

Durant, Will. *The Story of Philosophy: The Lives and Opinions of the World's Greatest Philosophers*. 2nd ed. New York: Pocket, 1991.

Ellis, James T. "American Catholics and the Intellectual Life." *Thought* 30.3 (1955) 351–88.

Ellul, Jacques. *The Political Illusion*. Translated by Konrad Kellen. New York: Alfred A. Knopf, 1967.

———. *Propaganda: The Formation of Men's Attitudes*. New York: Vintage, 1973.

———. *Violence: Reflections from a Christian Perspective*. New York: Seabury, 1969.

Etheridge, J. W., ed. "Targum Pseudo-Jonathan in English." In *The Targums of Onkelos and Jonathan Ben Uzziel on the Pentateuch: With the Fragments of the Jerusalem Targum*. London: Longman, Green, Longman, and Roberts, 1862.

Evagrius Ponticus. *Chapters on Prayer*. Translated by John Eudes Bamberger. Spencer, MA: Cistercian, 1972.

Falque, Emmanuel. *Crossing the Rubicon: The Borderlands of Philosophy and Theology*. Translated by Ruben Shank. New York: Fordham University Press, 2016.

———. *The Wedding Feast of the Lamb: Eros, the Body, and the Eucharist*. Translated by George Hughes. New York: Fordham University Press, 2016.

Fennell, Marylouise. "Faith and Law: Presidents and Trustees." In *Proceedings of What We Hold in Trust Seminar*. Notre Dame, IN: McGrath Institute for Church Life, 2009.

"Fiduciary Behavior: What's the Responsible Trustee to Do (and Not Do)?" *Trusteeship* 21.2 (2013) 8–16.

Flannery, Austin, ed. "Gaudium et Spes: Pastoral Constitution on the Church in the Modern World." In *Vatican Council II: Constitutions, Decrees, Declarations*, 163–282. Rev. ed. Northport, NY: Costello, 1996.

Flew, Anthony. *There Is a God: How the World's Most Notorious Atheist Changed His Mind*. New York: HarperOne, 2009.

Flipper, Joseph. *Between Apocalypse and Eschaton: History and Eternity in Henri de Lubac*. Minneapolis: Fortress, 2015.

Francis. *Evangelii Gaudium: The Joy of the Gospel*. Washington, DC: United States Conference of Catholic Bishops, 2013.

———. "Laudato Si." Encyclical delivered in Rome, May 24, 2015. http://w2.vatican.va/content/francesco/en/encyclicals/documents/papa-francesco_20150524_enciclica-laudato-si.html.

———. "To Participants in the Conference Promoted by the Pontifical Council for Justice and Peace on 'Impact Investing for the Poor.'" Speech delivered in Clementine Hall, Rome, June 16, 2014. https://w2.vatican.va/content/francesco/en/speeches/2014/june/documents/papa-francesco_20140616_convegno-justpeace.html.

Gallin, Alice, ed. *American Catholic Higher Education: Essential Documents, 1967–1990*. Notre Dame, IN: University of Notre Dame Press, 1992.

———. *Independence and a New Partnership in Catholic Higher Education*. Notre Dame, IN: University of Notre Dame Press, 1996.

———. *Negotiating Identity: Catholic Higher Education since 1969*. Notre Dame, IN: University of Notre Dame Press, 2000.

Garrigou-Lagrange, Reginald. "La Nouvelle Théologie Où Va-t-Elle?" *Angelicum* 23 (1946) 126–45.

Giussani, Luigi. *The Journey to Truth Is an Experience*. Montreal: McGill-Queen's University Press, 2006.

Gleason, Philip. *Contending with Modernity: Catholic Higher Education in the Twentieth Century*. New York: Oxford University Press, 1995.

Graden, John J. *Near Death Experiences of Doctors and Scientists*. n.p.: ITBD International, 2013.

Gritsch, E. *The Wit of Martin Luther*. Minneapolis: Fortress, 2002.

Grove, Kevin. "A Pondering Heart: The Immaculate Conception and the Sorrowful Mother in the Theology of Basil Moreau." In *Mary on the Eve of the Second Vatican Council*, edited by John C. Cavadini and Danielle M. Peters, 229–44. Notre Dame, IN: University of Notre Dame Press, 2017.

Hadot, Pierre. *Philosophy as a Way of Life*. Hoboken, NJ: Wiley-Blackwell, 1995.

———. *What Is Ancient Philosophy?* Translated by Michael Chase. Cambridge, MA: Harvard Belknap, 2004.

Halpin, Colleen. "The Pondering Heart: Notre Dame's Special Consecration to Our Lady." *Church Life Journal*. October 7, 2017. https://churchlife.nd.edu/2017/10/07/the-pondering-heart-notre-dames-special-consecration-to-our-lady.

Halvorson, Hans. "Quantum Mechanics and the Soul." In *The Soul Hypothesis: Investigations into the Existence of the Soul*, edited by Mark C. Baker and Stewart Goetz, 138–67. New York: Bloomsbury Academic, 2010.

Hays, Richard. *Reading Backwards: Figural Christology and the Fourfold Gospel Witness*. Waco, TX: Baylor University Press, 2016.

Heisenberg, Werner. *Physics and Beyond: Encounters and Conversatons*. New York: Harper and Row, 1971.

Heller, Michael. *Creative Tension: Essays on Science and Religion*. Philadelphia: Templeton Foundation, 2003.

Hesburgh, Theodore, ed. *The Challenge and Promise of a Catholic University*. Notre Dame, IN: University of Notre Dame Press, 1994.

The Holy Bible: Revised Standard Version, Catholic Edition. San Francisco, CA: Ignatius Press, 1966.

Horgan, John. *The End of Science*. New York: Addison-Wesley, 1996.

Hughes, Austin L. *The Folly of Scientism*. Unpublished, n.d.

Ibn Abu Hatam. *Tafsir Al-Qur'an Al-'Azim*. Edited by As'ad Muhammad al-Tayyib. Riyadh: Maktaba Nazar Mustafa al-Baz, 1419.

Ibn al-Jawzi, Abu al-Faraj 'Abd al-Rahman ibn 'Ali. *Zad Al-Masir Fi Ilm Al-Tafsir*. 4 vols. DKI, 2002.

International Theological Commission. "Message of the International Theological Commission on the Occasion of the Year of Faith." October 16, 2012. http://www.vatican.va/roman_curia/congregations/cfaith/cti_documents/rc_cti_20121016_messaggio-anno-fede_en.html.

Irenaeus of Lyons. *Against Heresies*. Edited by Alexander Roberts, et al. Louisville: Ex Fontibus, 2012.

Jacob of Serugh. *On Abraham and His Types*. Vol. 4. of *Homilae Selectae Mar-Jacobi Sarugensis*. Edited by P. Bedjan. Paris: Harrassowitz, 1905.

Jaki, Stanley L. *The Road of Science and the Ways to God*. Chicago: University of Chicago Press, 1978.

Jenkins, John I. "Land O'Lakes 50 Years On." *America* 217.2 (2017). https://www.americamagazine.org/faith/2017/07/11/document-changed-catholic-education-forever

John Paul II. "Centesimus Annus." Delivered in Rome, May 1, 1991. http://w2.vatican.va/content/john-paul-ii/en/encyclicals/documents/hf_jp-ii_enc_01051991_centesimus-annus.html.

———. "Deep Harmony Which Unites the Truths of Science with the Truths of Faith." Delivered in Rome, November 10, 1979. http://inters.org/John-Paul-II-deep-harmony.

———. "Ex Corde Ecclesiae." Delivered in Rome, August 15, 1990. http://w2.vatican.va/content/john-paul-ii/en/apost_constitutions/documents/hf_jp-ii_apc_15081990_ex-corde-ecclesiae.html.

———. "Redemptoris Custos: On the Person and Mission of Saint Joseph in the Life of Christ and of the Church." Delivered in Rome, August 15, 1989. http://w2.vatican.va/content/john-paul-ii/en/apost_exhortations/documents/hf_jp-ii_exh_15081989_redemptoris-custos.html.

———. *Sapientia Christiana*. Vatican: Libreria Editrice Vaticana, 1979.

Johnson, George. *Strange Beauty: Murray Gell-Mann and the Revolution in Twentieth-Century Physics*. New York: Random House, 2010.

Kant, Immanuel. *Religion within the Boundaries of Pure Reason*. Translated by Allen Wood and George DiGiovanni. New York: Cambridge University Press, 1998.

Keyishian v. Board of Regents, 385 US 589 (Jan. 23, 1967). http://law2.umkc.edu/faculty/projects/ftrials/conlaw/Keyishian.html.

Kilpatrick, Peter. "The College of Engineering at Notre Dame and Its Interaction with Its Catholic Mission and the New Notre Dame Institute for Advanced Studies." In *The Idea of a Catholic Institute for Advanced Study*, edited by Vittorio Hösle and Donald L. Stelluto. Notre Dame, IN: Notre Dame Institute for Advanced Study.

King, Herbert, ed. *Joseph Kentenich—Collected Texts: Free and Wholly Human.* Vallendar, Germany: Schönstatt-Patres, 2004.

Kulayni, Muhammad b. Yaʻqub. *Al-Kafi.* Tehran: Dar al-Kutub al-Islamiyya, 1408.

Leclercq, Jean. *The Love of Learning and the Desire for God: A Study of Monastic Culture.* New York: Fordham University Press, 1982.

Lemaitre, Georges. "The Beginning of the World from the Point of View of Quantum Theory." *Nature* 127 (1931) 706.

Lonergan, Bernard. *Insight: A Study of Human Understanding.* Edited by F. E. Crowe and R. M. Doran. Collected Works of Bernard Lonergan 3. Toronto: University of Toronto Press, 1992.

Luria, Maxwell S., and Richard L. Hoffman, eds. *Middle English Lyrics.* New York: W.W. Norton, 1974.

Luther, Martin. *Luthers Werke: Kritische Gesamtausgabe.* Weimar: Böhlau, 1883.

Lynch, Robert G. *Exceptional Returns: Economic, Fiscal, and Social Benefits of Investment in Early Childhood Development.* Washington, DC: Economic Policy Institute, 2014.

MacIntyre, Alasdair. *God, Philosophy, Universities: A Selective History of the Catholic Philosophical Tradition.* Reprint. Lanham, MD: Rowman & Littlefield, 2011.

Marion, Jean-Luc. *Believing in Order to See: On the Rationality of Revelation and the Irrationality of Some Believers.* Translated by Christina M. Gschwandtner. New York: Fordham University Press, 2017.

———. *On Descartes's Passive Thought: The Myth of Cartesian Dualism.* Translated by Christina Gschwandtner. Chicago: University of Chicago Press, 2018.

———. *Prolegomena to Charity.* Translated by Stephen Lewis. New York: Fordham University Press, 2002.

Marsden, George M. *The Soul of the American University: From Protestant Establishment to Established Nonbelief.* New York: Oxford University Press, 1994.

Mayr, Ernst. "Teleological and Teleonomic, A New Analysis." In *Methodological and Historical Essays in the Natural and Social Sciences,* edited by R. S. Cohen and M. W. Wartofsky, 91–117. Dordrecht: D. Reidel, 1974.

McBrien, Richard P. "Students, Faculty, and Administrators." In *Proceedings of What We Hold in Trust Seminar.* Notre Dame, IN: McGrath Institute for Church Life, 2009.

Melitos of Sardis. "Fragment of Paschal Homily." In *Second-Century Christianity: A Collection of Fragments,* edited by Robert M. Grant, 32. Louisville: Westminster John Knox, 2003.

Milbank, John. *The Word Made Strange: Theology, Language, and Culture.* Malden, MA: Blackwell, 1998.

Milbank, John, and Adrian Pabst. *The Politics of Virtue: Post-Liberalism and the Human Future.* New York: Rowman & Littlefield, 2016.

Moreau, Basil. "Christian Education." In *Basil Moreau: Essential Writings,* edited by Kevin Grove and Andrew Gawrych, 329–76. Notre Dame, IN: Ave Maria, 2014.

Moreau, Basil. "Circular Letter 36." In *Basil Moreau: Essential Writings,* edited by Kevin Grove and Andrew Gawrych, 415–23. Notre Dame, IN: Ave Maria, 2014.

Morey, Melanie M. "The Way We Are: The Present Relationship of Religious Congregations of Women to the Colleges They Founded." In *Catholic Women's Colleges in America,* edited by Tracy Schier and Cynthia Russett, 277–324. Baltimore: Johns Hopkins University Press, 2002.

Morey, Melanie M., and John J Piderit. *Catholic Higher Education: A Culture in Crisis.* New York: Oxford University Press, 2006.

Moskowitz, Peter. *How to Kill a City: Gentrification, Inequality, and the Fight for the Neighborhood.* New York: Nation, 2017.

Newman, John Henry. *The Idea of a University.* Edited by Martin Svaglic. Notre Dame, IN: University of Notre Dame Press, 1986.

Norris, Robert S., and Hans M. Kristensen. "Global Nuclear Weapons Inventories, 1945–2010." *Bulletin of the Atomic Scientists* 66.4 (2010) 77–83.

O'Brien, George Dennis. *The Idea of a Catholic University.* Chicago: University of Chicago Press, 2002.

O'Connor, Edward D., ed. *The Dogma of the Immaculate Conception.* Notre Dame, IN: University of Notre Dame Press, 1958.

O'Regan, Cyril. *The Anatomy of Misremembering: Von Balthasar's Response to Philosophical Modernity.* New York: Herder and Herder, 2014.

"Of Beauty and Consolation Episode 9 Edward Witten." YouTube video. 1:28:27. July 21, 2014. https://www.youtube.com/watch?v=RfwsvSjXkJU&t=908s.

Origen. "Commentary on John 1.4(6)." In *The Commentary of Origen on St. John's Gospel,* edited by A. E. Brooke, 7. Vol. 1. Cambridge: Cambridge University Press, 1896.

———. *Contra Celsum.* Translated by Henry Chadwick. Cambridge: Cambridge University Press, 1965.

———. "De principiis 4.3.13." In *Origenes vier Bücher von den Prinzipien,* edited by H. Görgemanns and H. Karpp, 772. Darmstadt: Wissenschaftliche Buchgesellschaft, 1992.

———. "Homily 16.6." In *Homélies sur S. Luc: Texte latin et fragments grecs (2ème édition revue et corrigée,* edited by H. Crouzel, et al. Sources chrétiennes 87. Paris: Editions du Cerf, 1998.

Paul VI. "Ecclesiam Suam." August 6, 1964. http://w2.vatican.va/content/paul-vi/en/encyclicals/documents/hf_p-vi_enc_06081964_ecclesiam.html.

———. "Populorum Progressio." March 26, 1967. http://w2.vatican.va/content/paul-vi/en/encyclicals/documents/hf_p-vi_enc_26031967_populorum.html.

Pelikan, J., and H. Lehmann, eds. *Luther's Wars.* Philadelphia: Fortress, 1955.

Pender, E .E. "Spiritual Pregnancy in Plato's 'Symposium.'" *The Classical Quarterly* 42.1 (1992) 72–86.

Peters, Danielle. *Ecce Educatrix Tua: The Role of the Blessed Virgin Mary for a Pedagogy of Holiness in the Thought of John Paul II and Father Joseph Kentenich.* Lanham, MD: University Press of America, 2009.

Pieper, Josef. *The Four Cardinal Virtues.* Notre Dame, IN: University of Notre Dame Press, 2014.

Pius X. "Ad Diem Illum Laetissimum." February 2, 1904. http://w2.vatican.va/content/pius-x/en/encyclicals/documents/hf_p-x_enc_02021904_ad-diem-illum-laetissimum.html.

Polanyi, Michael. "The Republic of Science: Its Political and Economic Theory." *Minerva* 38.1 (2000) 1–21.

Pontifical Council for Justice and Peace. *Compendium of the Social Doctrine of the Church.* Washington, DC: USCCB, 2005.

The Quran. Translated by M. A. S. Abdel Haleem. Oxford: Oxford University Press, 2005.

Ratzinger, Joseph. *Introduction to Christianity.* 2nd ed. San Francisco: Ignatius, 2004.

———. *The Spirit of the Liturgy.* San Francisco: Ignatius, 2000.

al-Razi, Fakhr al-Din. *Mafatih Al-Ghayb.* Beirut: Dar Ihya' al-Turath al-'Arabi, 1420.

Robinson, Jonathan. *In No Strange Land: The Embodied Mysticism of Saint Philip Neri.* Kettering, OH: Angelico, 2015.

Rothman, Noah C. "The Fatalist Conceit." *Commentary* 145.5 (2018) 15–20.

Rubin, Miri. *Mother of God: A History of the Virgin Mary.* New Haven, CT: Yale University Press, 2009.

Rutler, George W. "The Idea of a Catholic University 50 Years After Land O'Lakes." *Crisis Magazine.* July 20, 2017. https://www.crisismagazine.com/2017/idea-university-50-years-land-olakes-statement.

Schönborn, Christoph. "The Designs of Science." *First Things: A Monthly Journal of Religion and Public Life* 159 (2006) 34–38.

Shiffman, Mark. "Humanity 4.5." *First Things: A Monthly Journal of Religion and Public Life* 257 (2015) 23–30.

Shipley, Joseph T. *The Origins of English Words: A Discursive Dictionary for Indo-European Roots.* Baltimore: Johns Hopkins University Press, 1984.

Smith, Christian, and John C. Cavadini. *Building Catholic Higher Education: Unofficial Reflections from the University of Notre Dame.* Eugene, OR: Cascade, 2014.

Spitzer, Robert J. *New Proofs for the Existence of God.* Grand Rapids, MI: Eerdmans, 2010.

Tabataba'i, Muhammad Husayn. *Tafsir Al-Mizan.* Vol. 1. http://www.islamicmobility.com//files/pdf/pdf326.pdf.

Thompson, Robert J. *Reason and Tolerance: The Purpose and Practice of Higher Education.* New York: Oxford University Press, 2014.

Tucker, Todd. *Notre Dame vs. the Klan: How the Fighting Irish Defeated the Klu Klux Klan.* Chicago: Loyola, 2004.

Tzamalikos, P. *Origen: Philosophy of History and Eschatology.* Leiden: Brill, 2007.

University of Notre Dame. "Mission Statement." https://www.nd.edu/about/mission-statement.

USCCB. *Co-Workers in the Vineyard of the Lord.* Washington, DC: USCCB, 2005.

———. *The Program of Priestly Formation.* Washington, DC: USCCB, 2005.

Wallace, William A. *The Modeling of Nature.* Washington, DC: Catholic University of America Press, 1996.

Ward, Graham. *The Politics of Discipleship: Becoming Postmaterial Citizens.* Grand Rapids: Eerdmans, 2009.

Watson, Francis. *The Fourfold Gospel: A Theological Reading of the New Testament Portraits of Jesus.* Grand Rapids: Baker Academic, 2016.

Weil, Simone. *Awaiting God: A New Translation of "Attente de Dieu and Lettre a Un Religieux."* Translated by Bradley Jersak. Maywood, CT: Fresh Wind Press, 2013.

———. *Waiting for God.* Translated by Emma Craufurd. New York: G. P. Putnam's, 1951.

Wellmon, Chad. "For Moral Clarity, Don't Look to Universities." *The Chronicle of Higher Education.* August 14, 2017. https://www.chronicle.com/article/For-Moral-Clarity-Dont-Look/240921.

Weyl, Hermann. *The Open World: Three Lectures on the Metaphysical Implications of Science.* New Haven, CT: Yale University Press, 1932.